WHO SAYS
I CAN'T?

WHO SAYS I CAN'T?

THE ASTONISHING STORY OF A FEARLESS LIFE

COACH ROB MENDEZ
WITH JOE LAYDEN

HARPER HORIZON

To my dad, Robert Sr.; mother, Josie; sisters, Jackie and Maddy; both tias, Tota and Cindy; and of course, my Grandpa Danny and Grandma Mona. I dedicate this book to my parents and the rest of my family for their belief in me, their support, and ultimately for bringing love and strength into my heart. My father was my biggest advocate for me growing up, not allowing for anyone else to see me any different and always reminding me to focus on what I am able to do, rather than what I'm not able to do. And my mother showed me that love is everything. She has a big heart and is my biggest supporter. I love you all very much, and I consider myself one of the luckiest individuals to grow up in the family I did.

CONTENTS

Prologue ix

Chapter One 1
Chapter Two 19
Chapter Three 37
Chapter Four 53
Chapter Five 75
Chapter Six 95
Chapter Seven 117
Chapter Eight 137
Chapter Nine 157
Chapter Ten 179
Chapter Eleven 195

Epilogue 217
Acknowledgments 229
About the Authors 231

PROLOGUE

AUGUST 26, 2018

It's funny the way a good day can turn bad without any warning. That is a fact of life for anyone, of course, but it's particularly true in my case.

Today is a beautiful summer Sunday in the Bay Area of Northern California, specifically in the town of Morgan Hill, where my parents live. I'm staying for the weekend, while my caretaker is out of town. I'm hanging out in the garage, just shooting the breeze with my dad as he does some work, the way we did while I was growing up. The sun is fading in the evening sky, and music is playing in the background. It's comfortable, familiar, peaceful.

Reflexively, I decide to check my phone. It sits in a cradle just below eye level on my elevated, motorized wheelchair. I lean forward to grab the stylus with my teeth. It's a simple maneuver, one I've executed thousands of times before, and I do it without a thought, like anyone else who compulsively plays with their smartphone. Just a couple of quick pecks, and I'm in sync with the digital world: answering texts and emails, checking Instagram and Twitter feeds, getting ready for my fantasy football draft.

You know, the usual stuff.

But something happens as I reach for the stylus. It registers first as a wave of disorientation. I'm used to feeling the firm snap of a safety belt holding me in place when I move too quickly or too far. And believe me, I do that a lot. I often thrash about in my chair, gesticulating with my head and shoulders, expressing emotion with what I have, rather than worrying about what I don't have. I lean and twist and turn, sometimes as a means of expression and sometimes in an attempt to alleviate the enormous strain that my spine bears all day, every day. For a guy stuck in a wheelchair, or maybe because I am stuck in a wheelchair, I have an abundance of energy. To minimize the chance of injury, my chair is equipped with two straps: one for the chest, and one for the waist. Much to the dismay of my friends and family, I rarely use the chest strap. Too confining. I figure the waist belt is sufficient. Usually it is.

Unless you forget to use it.

You know how they say everything slows down when you're in an accident? Well, it's true. I can feel myself leaning forward, and at some point, I realize there is nothing to stop the progression. My head goes right past the stylus and the phone, and my torso dutifully follows. I am out of the chair now, hurtling—can that possibly be the right word when falling from a height of only four feet? Yes, it seems exactly right—toward the garage floor. I can see the concrete rising to greet me. The feeling of helplessness is impressive, if not overwhelming. I can do nothing to stop the impending catastrophe. I have no arms to break the fall, no legs to absorb some of the impact. I turn my head to the side.

And close my eyes.

• • •

I wake in the passenger seat of my father's Chevy Suburban. His hands are locked on the steering wheel, his eyes red and wet. We are racing down the interstate, toward Saint Louise Regional Hospital.

"Dad, it's okay. I'm all right."

This is not true. My head throbs. My face is on fire. Liquid drips into my left eye, sticky and stinging.

"Please, Robert," he says. "Be still."

I look down. Blood is everywhere: on the seat, on my clothes. I blink hard, trying to clear my vision. I know I'm hurt, and though I don't know exactly how bad, I'm worried not only about my health but what my injuries might mean for the new direction my life has taken.

Right now, though, I mainly feel bad for my father, who has been through so much with me—and who taught me never to focus on what I couldn't do but rather on what I could—and how he will process all of this. Bad enough to see your only son's head smack against a concrete floor with the sickening sound of a pancake being slapped against a griddle (that's exactly the way my father would later describe it). But to wonder whether you'd buckled his seat belt, or buckled it effectively, was even worse.

It could have happened to anyone. Anytime. And, ultimately, it's my responsibility. I am not a child. I am a grown man, thirty years old. But in that moment, there is no consoling my father.

"Don't worry, Dad."

He doesn't respond. He simply cries.

At the hospital he whisks me into the emergency room, carrying me like a toddler against his chest and shoulder. It's a head injury—the kind that gets you pushed right to the front of the line at the ER. Within minutes, I'm surrounded by doctors and nurses cleaning my wounds and assessing the damage, conversing calmly but forcefully in the staccato rhythm of trauma care. The pain ebbs and flows as they wheel me through the hospital for X-rays and a CAT scan. Six stiches are required to close the gash above my left eye, but of greater concern are the fractures to my orbital bone and cheekbone. The doctors say I'm lucky. It could have been worse. A face-first plant would have shattered my nose. Had I turned too far to the side—a natural and perfectly reasonable response of self-preservation—I could have struck my temple. If that had happened, I might not have even made it to the hospital.

So, yeah, I got off easy.

"When can I go home?" Before anyone can answer, waves of nausea rock me. I start vomiting. And I don't stop until the meds kick in a few hours later.

I'm discharged at seven o'clock the next morning. My head is still throbbing, my neck aches so badly I can barely move, and my face feels as though it's been rubbed raw with sandpaper. They tell me the obvious: I've suffered considerable damage, including a concussion, and that while the outcome could have been worse, I'm going to feel lousy for a while.

"Take it easy," one of the docs suggests. "No work."

"For how long?"

"At least a couple weeks."

My heart sinks. For twelve years I've been coaching high school and Pop Warner football in the Bay Area, and now, finally, I have a team of my own. I'm the head junior varsity (JV) coach at Prospect High School in nearby Saratoga. Classes have already begun; our first preseason game is only a few days away.

Two weeks?

"No way," I respond. "I need to get back on the sideline. Now."

Not advisable, the doctor reiterates. "You just can't."

I don't argue. There's no point. But I can hear the voice in my head, the one I listen to above all others. And I smile.

Who says I can't?!

WHO SAYS I CAN'T?

CHAPTER ONE

CHAPTER ONE

Let's get the technical stuff out of the way. I was born with tetra-amelia syndrome, a rare congenital disorder that prevents the formation of limbs during embryonic development. How rare? Extraordinarily rare. There are, supposedly, only a dozen or so people in the world currently living with tetra-amelia. I don't know if this is true. To be honest, I have my doubts. I presume there are at least a handful of people in underdeveloped nations, far from the glare of Western media, who are coping with tetra-amelia. But that doesn't lessen its uniqueness. To me, statistics are irrelevant, and probability feels arbitrary.

This is my life, and it always has been. I know nothing else. That's one of the reasons I've always been a little uncomfortable with other people defining me by my appearance or by my physical limitations. I don't think of myself as a football coach without limbs; I am, simply, a football coach. In recent years I've received a fair amount of attention, thanks in large part to a feature story in *ESPN The Magazine* and an ESPN-produced documentary (also called *Who Says I Can't?*), as well as my having received the Jimmy V Award for Perseverance at the 2019 ESPY Awards.

At first, I found the spotlight somewhat disorienting— so many people telling me I'm an inspiration because of the way I deal with a significant physical challenge. I get it. I feel honored that anyone would look at me that way, and I am grateful and humbled to be in a position to help others who might be struggling to overcome hardship. At the same time, I'd be lying if I said I feel heroic. I don't know what it's like to have arms and legs. I don't know what it's like to walk or run. To me, far more heroic is the person who has these functions and then, through illness or injury or accident, loses them and somehow overcomes the grief and pain and gets on with his or her life.

If I lost my eyesight tomorrow, or my hearing . . . man, I can't imagine how I would deal with it. What I have now is what I've always had. What I don't have . . . well, it's hard to miss what you've never experienced.

Don't get me wrong. I'm not suggesting that I don't have bad days. Sometimes I get angry or frustrated. I'm a football coach. I love sports. I wonder what it would be like to throw a ball. I wonder what it would be like to hold the people I love, to touch them with my hands, rather than my shoulders or face. Not long ago, one of the players on my football team had a panic attack after a game. His body started cramping, and he got scared. I wanted to embrace him, to physically reassure him that everything would be all right. But I couldn't do that. All I could do was talk to him from my chair and ask others for help. More practically, I'd like to not be dependent on someone else for the daily functions that most people take for granted. I'd like to be able to take a shower and dress myself in the morning. I'd like to be able to feed myself.

Frankly? Bluntly? I'd like to be able to wipe myself after going to the bathroom.

There are days, too, when soreness escalates into pain, and that's a legitimate challenge to the psyche, as it is for anyone who lives with chronic discomfort. I'm stuck in a wheelchair all day. That, alone, can be problematic. But I also have developed scoliosis related to tetra-amelia. It's not only that I lack the legs and lower buttocks to help distribute and support the weight of my upper body. There is also the issue of proportions: my head is normal-size, but my torso is smaller than normal. This puts inordinate stress on my spine. I do a lot of stretching. I get physical therapy. Some days I feel pretty good. Other days I hurt. A lot.

That's not a sob story. It's not even a complaint. It's just the truth. But I love my life, and I believe that I have been put on this planet, in this condition, for a purpose. And I embrace that purpose with all my heart. I want to use my platform (funny, it wasn't so long ago that I didn't even know I had a platform!) and this book—the story of my life—to help others in any way I can. In the last year, in addition to working full-time as a football coach and teacher's aide, I've addressed hundreds of people face-to-face at speaking engagements across the country. I've also been profiled by multiple media outlets, giving me the opportunity to have an impact on millions of people.

It's been a wild ride, to be sure, and it's taken some getting used to, but I'm glad that I've been able to inspire people to live their lives to the fullest and love themselves for who they are. And it's something I want to keep doing. This is my calling. This is God's plan for me. I see that now, and I am grateful.

• • •

I was a happy kid. People sometimes have a hard time believing that, yet it's true. From day one I was nurtured by a badass family that gave me endless love and support but never allowed me to feel sorry for myself or let others place restrictions on what I could do. I know it wasn't easy for them. My parents, Robert and

Josie Mendez, didn't know of my impending physical challenges until the eighth month of pregnancy. That's not much time to process the daunting prospect of raising a child born without limbs, of bringing into the world a little boy whose future was, at best, uncertain.

Imagine what it must have been like: months of joyful preparation and excitement, a young couple eagerly anticipating the birth of their second child (my sister, Jackie, was three years old when I was born). Then, suddenly, it's as though they're the object of some cosmic practical joke, or a test of biblical proportions. During a routine visit a doctor tells them something is amiss. There are tests and sonograms, and finally the news is broken.

No arms.

No legs.

I've thought about this from time to time, how my parents felt when that news was delivered. Doesn't almost every father dream of playing catch with his son? Doesn't almost every mother want to feel the warmth of her baby's arms wrapped around her neck? What is it like to be hit with the realization, stark and cold, that these things won't be part of your child's life, of your life together with him? In that instant, I would imagine, you feel a mix of sadness and anger, of being cheated. Mostly, though, I would imagine you feel incalculable empathy for your unborn child. I'm not a parent, but I know that the one thing all parents want is to shield their child from pain. That day in the doctor's office, my mother and father were told there would be no shielding.

I was different. Pain, in all its myriad forms, would be a fundamental part of my existence. Mom and Dad couldn't chase it away. All they could do was help me learn how to cope with it.

In many ways, I grew up like other children, which meant that regarding events predating my arrival on the planet, information was dispensed on a need-to-know basis. I heard lots of stories and family history, most often shared by grandparents and aunts and uncles, but this particular subject—the day my parents were told their son would be one in a billion—they kept to themselves.

I come from a tight-knit family, made even tighter by the shared ordeal of raising a child with serious physical challenges. My mother was and is the sweetest person I have ever known; she wears her emotions on her sleeve. My dad is more stoic, but when I was a little boy, he was my best friend and most vocal advocate. If ever there was a time when my parents experienced anger or depression or self-pity over being burdened with a child born without limbs, I didn't see it. They never felt sorry for themselves, and they didn't indulge any of my self-pity.

"You can do anything you want, Robert," they always said. And I believed them.

When I first viewed the ESPN documentary, however, I truly understood the burden my parents carried—the fear and doubt and shock they experienced that day in the doctor's office, and how it carried over for some time afterward.

My mother said, "I didn't have a choice to have an abortion, so I had to . . . keep Robert," leaving these words open to interpretation.

As the camera rolled, I watched my dad stare into the distance, his face carrying the weight of an event thirty years in the past just as clearly as if it happened yesterday.

"In the back of my mind, I'm asking, Why? Why my son?" he said. "You know, less than one hundred born like him in the world."

No handbook exists for something like this. I suppose you just hope and pray everything turns out all right, that fear and anger will be eclipsed by love. That seems to have been the case for me, and it's just one of many reasons I consider myself a lucky man. Those frightened, stunned parents in the documentary? Until that moment, I'd never seen them, never known them. I'm proud of them for being honest in the documentary, and I have even greater respect and admiration for them now. We were both given a life sentence, after all, and the extent to which mine would be tolerable, miserable, or filled with joy was largely their determination. I've been called "inspirational" and "heroic," but if I live up to those descriptions, even for a moment, it's only because I had strong role models.

From their perspective, it seemed I had accepted the situation I was born into, and there was no reason to dredge up gloomier times. It's cliché, of course, but we lived day by day, and we made the best of it. My parents weren't going to go back and cry and complain about what might have been. There was no point.

That's how I learned my way of going about things. I think of myself as compassionate. I have empathy for people who struggle for whatever reasons. But I admit I have a low tolerance for complainers. That's not because I believe I have it harder than anyone else—we all have challenges, and we all experience good and bad days. It's more about the way I was raised. My parents and grandparents and siblings all worked hard, and they all managed to figure things out. If you encountered an obstacle, you didn't whine or cry; you did your best to overcome that obstacle. Whether it was taking me to an amusement park or just carrying my wheelchair on and off the family van, they soldiered on. Quietly. Resolutely.

Consequently, I rarely found myself consumed by the question everyone assumes I must have asked: "Why am I like this?" As a little boy, at least, I never had a burning curiosity to know whether my differences (and I always viewed them as *differences*, not shortcomings) were a tragic miscalculation by God, or part of his master plan. I didn't ask my parents for an explanation, and none was offered. As a family, we kept the oars in the water, pulling together as one, driving endlessly against the current.

. . .

I was born at Santa Clara Valley Medical Center in San Jose; a team of doctors from Stanford assisted in the procedure, in the event of complications. It isn't easy to find medical experts who have experience with tetra-amelia, and most babies who are born with it live only a few days. Those who do survive typically have significant cognitive and intellectual impairment along with the physical challenges. It isn't a life anyone would wish for themselves or their child. I survived those first few days, and before long, the doctors realized I had no cognitive or other physical deficiencies. However narrow my world might be, it would be accessible to the fullest extent possible for someone with tetra-amelia.

There was hope, and my parents grasped it.

When I was eighteen months old, our family was put in touch with an adaptive physical education teacher in the Gilroy School District, where I lived.

"Focus on the positive things in his life," they were told. "Don't focus on the limitations. He can breathe, he has a brain, he has a penis. That's all he needs."

Amen to that.

My father was a carpenter, who later returned to school and became a respiratory therapist. My mother stayed at home to take care of me, obviously a full-time job. At the urging of therapists and doctors, I was enrolled in a preschool at under two years of age.

"Robert needs to be integrated into life," they said. "The sooner, the better."

I would imagine this pushed against my parents' natural inclination to protect me from all the terrible things that can happen to any child, let alone one without arms or legs. But they were adamant that I wouldn't be treated as a freak, or even as a little boy more breakable than his peers. They wanted for me what every parent wants for their child: happiness, normalcy.

If anyone used certain buzzwords around us, my father would get righteously pissed off. He never saw me as "disabled" and always pushed for me to be in the mainstream at school. Because I look different and my condition is so unique, people sometimes assumed I suffered from intellectual shortcomings. This wasn't the case, and my dad made sure everyone knew it, in the same way he fought to prevent me from being marginalized. There was the time, for example, when someone suggested that my parents enter me in a wheelchair soccer league, since I loved sports so much.

"Screw that!" I remember my dad shouting. "He doesn't need to be segregated."

My father also hated the word *special*. He preferred *unique*, and he would frequently tell me that uniqueness had less to do with any physical differences than it did with something intangible: a person's spirit. Mine, he said, was immeasurable, almost from the beginning.

When I was born, in that instant I slid out of my mother and into the world, my father must have felt a deeply confusing and disorienting set of emotions. But you know what he used to tell me?

"Robert, I could hear 'Bad to the Bone' playing in my head."

You know that song, by George Thorogood and the Destroyers? It's been played in a hundred television shows and movies, and it serves as the unofficial soundtrack for a wide array of athletes and tough guys. Against a teeth-rattling guitar riff, the song opens in a hospital, with the nurses marveling at a particularly impressive newborn. But the wise head nurse cautions everyone to keep their distance:

> She could tell right away
> That I was bad to the bone!

That's the way my dad spun it. I wasn't just a happy kid, I was a tough kid, born without some basic equipment but blessed with some other equally important tools. He was right, even if his response was sometimes a bit too animated. That was just my dad. He was a warrior, and he saw me as a warrior as well. I presume some people thought he was crazy, but his heart has always been in the right place, and I'm lucky to have him in my corner. Just as I'm lucky to have my mother and my two sisters, and the rest of a large extended family. They all like to say I was "an easy kid." Imagine that! There is nothing "easy" about caring for someone with tetra-amelia. Yet, for some reason, some unfathomable leveling of the playing field, it wasn't in my nature to be depressed or angry, which I guess took some of the pain out of the equation for my parents, and for me.

Home movies rarely tell a comprehensive story, but you'll have a hard time finding any video from my childhood in which I'm not smiling or laughing or telling jokes. Rather than relying on others to cart me from room to room, I used to roll around the house or waddle on my butt, almost as quickly as everyone else could walk. I don't remember feeling deprived or cheated in any way.

"Robert has a gift that doesn't require him to be physical," my father told ESPN. "And I think he just took the ball and ran. He's different. Even today. He sees people staring as an opportunity."

This is true. I do see it as an opportunity, a chance to change people's perceptions of what is and isn't normal, and to help others push through the barriers that life can place in front of us. But if I have this attitude, it's mainly because I was lucky to be born with it as a coping mechanism and to have it reinforced by my family.

• • •

I never lacked for companionship. When I was growing up, our house, on a pleasant cul-de-sac in Gilroy, always seemed to be filled with relatives—not just parents and siblings but an assortment of grandparents, aunts, uncles, and cousins.

My older sister, Jackie, was my first and best friend, simply because she was always around and apparently had the patience of a saint. It was Jackie who taught me how to play video games. I have only the dimmest memory of when it began, but I've heard stories from everyone in my family about how I was three or four years old, sitting on the couch next to Jackie, watching wide eyed as she played *Zelda* and *Super Mario* on Nintendo. She was only six or seven at the time. I don't know if she was any good at video games, but she seemed to be enjoying it, and I wanted to be part of the fun.

"Can I try?"

Unfazed, Jackie said, "Sure," and wedged the controller between my upper chest and chin. Looking back on it now, it's wild to think about how creative and thoughtful she was, even at such a young age.

"Try to press the buttons with your chin." I did as she suggested, and the characters and vehicles on the television screen responded. Not very well, but still, they moved when I told them to move. I had control. What a miracle!

"Good job!"

Just like that, I was hooked on video games. I couldn't walk or run in real life, but I could pretend. I could use the characters on the screen as surrogates. In a sense, my world had opened up. I practiced every day, figuring out ways to use my chin and neck and shoulders to manipulate the controls, and eventually I got good enough to play against Jackie. I discovered that I was a competitive kid. Sometimes my sister would let me win, and sometimes she wouldn't. Sometimes I beat her straight up.

I guess you could say Jackie was my first coach.

But I didn't hide in the house, relying solely on family for friendship and love and understanding. Mine isn't a story of ostracization or bullying, or of an outsider trying to force his way in.

My neighbor Alex started coming over to my house regularly when we were in preschool. He and another childhood buddy, Abed. They remain friends of mine to this day. A key to our friendship, I think, is that they never treated me with pity. We played video games together, watched TV, and had disagreements, like all kids. They knew I was different, but that difference didn't define or hinder our friendship. If anything, it may have strengthened it. I remember one day, hanging out in Alex's backyard with him and Abed and some other kids. Alex's family had a pool, and all the kids were playing in the water. I imagine there was adult supervision somewhere—we couldn't have been more than nine or ten years old—but it wasn't exactly vigilant. I was sitting in my chair on the patio, and Alex yelled to me.

"Hey, Rob. You want to come in?"

Here's what I thought: "Hell yeah, I want to come in!"

Here's what I said: "No, my mom won't let me."

Alex smiled, as if to say, "Your mom's not here." I smiled back. The next thing I knew, he was leaning over me, unhooking my safety belt and lifting me out of the wheelchair. He carried me into the shallow end of the pool, where the other kids greeted us. They passed me around gently, let me lie back in the water and float safely in their arms, as if cradled in a human net. The water felt so clean and fresh. So free!

This was what it was like for me as a kid: surrounded by family and good friends who never wanted me to feel left out. A lot of people presume that my childhood, and particularly my adolescence, must have been brutal. Kids are vicious, right? Surely, they would have picked on the boy with no limbs. But this wasn't my experience. I'm not saying no one whispered about me when I wasn't around; nor am I saying everyone liked me. But most of the time I was happy, and the reason for that was because I was blessed to have friends and family who cared about me and who did their best to ensure I wasn't ostracized, intentionally or otherwise.

I was loved, and I knew it.

CHAPTER TWO

There is a truth and an irony to my life that is irrefutable: I cannot play sports, yet sports are one of my greatest passions.

As middle school approached, at ten to twelve years old, this did become a source of significant disappointment. Everyone did their best to mitigate the frustration. My father played in a softball league in Salinas, and he'd bring me to games and let me fill out his team's lineup card in the dugout. I'm sure he changed things before the first pitch, but this simple exercise provided me with the satisfaction of being involved, and I loved him for it. Similarly, my uncle put me on the Little League team he coached. This allowed me to go to practices and hang out with my cousins, who were on the team, which was fun, even if I couldn't do more than cheer. The first year, unfortunately, the league wouldn't allow me to sit in the dugout during games. The stated reason was liability issues.

What if he gets hit by a foul ball?

What if someone throws a bat, and it clips him in the head?

What if he falls out of his chair?

So I watched from the stands, which in some ways was worse than not being there at all. I put up with this nonsense for one season. Then, with the help of my father and my uncle, I fought back.

"This isn't fair," I said. "I'm part of this team. I should be in the dugout with my friends."

We reached a compromise: I could sit in the dugout with my teammates, provided I wore a batting helmet at all times. This seemed a little excessive, but I accepted it. At least I was with my teammates. More importantly, I had learned the value of standing up for myself and fighting for what I believed was right.

I've always loved sports. My father insists that the first word I ever spoke was *ball*. True? I don't know. Makes for a good story though.

On weekends we'd visit my grandparents' house. My grandfather Danny Mendez was a diehard fan of every professional sports team in the Bay Area, including the San Francisco 49ers, and he used to tell me stories about the team's glory days of the 1970s and '80s.

"Joe Montana was the greatest quarterback ever," he'd say. "And Steve Young wasn't too bad either."

Grandpa wasn't merely a fan. He knew the game, and he'd break it down for me by position. He'd sit me on his lap, and we'd watch games together, while he explained what happened on every play. I got my love of football from my grandfather. I picked up a few other things along the way as well. It's funny how much someone can teach you without even trying, simply by going through his life, day after day, with integrity and love.

My grandfather was born in California, the son of Mexican immigrants. He embodied the American dream. He married my grandmother Ramona at a young age, and together they raised three children in a comfortable suburban home in Salinas.

My grandmother was a stay-at-home mom; my grandfather worked, hard. (Not that raising children isn't hard!) Grandpa Danny's primary job, one he held for more than forty years, was custodian for the Salinas Unified School District. He loved kids. And I don't say that casually. We all remember what it was like to be in school. We remember the teachers, administrators, coaches, and support staff—some of whom seemed to genuinely love their work—and the endless, overwhelming human interaction that came with it. I was a teenager once, and while I wasn't a bad kid, I wasn't a picnic either. (Who is?) I'm currently a coach who works with teens. It can be a joyous, confusing, frustrating time of life. I think a lot of adults who work with kids forget that and lose sight of why they got into the field in the first place.

My grandfather didn't become a school custodian because he wanted to work with kids; that just happened to be a fringe benefit. I remember numerous times when I'd be out in public with my grandparents, and we'd bump into someone at a grocery store or a shopping mall or a sporting event. Everyone seemed to know him and love him. From students to teachers to parents, they'd run up to Grandpa Danny and hug him and shake his hand, ask how he was doing. And he'd proudly introduce me to them. With the kids, especially, he was loose and natural. He would joke around with them, but he'd also express genuine interest in their lives.

Custodians often pass unnoticed in the halls of public schools, but not Grandpa Danny. He was a *presence.* You know why? Because he cared.

I've tried to carve out my own place in the world. While it's fine and normal for a kid to have heroes and to dream of being a professional athlete or an actor or a musician, or almost anyone who seems to have found fame and success through honorable means, the people most often responsible for shaping our lives are usually closer to home. I've always been determined to write my own story, but if I could choose one person whose spirit and outlook most reflects my own, especially when it comes to dealing positively with young people, it would be my grandpa.

Sometimes when I talk to my players, I can almost hear his voice. It's not that I'm trying to be their buddy—that's not my job—but I do want them to know that I love them and care about them. I don't value their opinions any less because they're children, and I don't discount the magnitude of their struggles, which are every bit as real as those we face as adults.

I was very close to my grandfather, but I got to know him even better after he died, when I sat at his funeral, crying and laughing as a litany of eulogists told stories about what made Grandpa Danny special. They all made note of his ability to connect with people, to make you feel like you were the most important person in his life, if only for a few moments.

"He didn't care who you were, how old or young you were, or where you came from, or what you did for a living," one of them said. "He treated you like a person."

When you work in a school district, you get exposed to various personalities and different types of kids, every day. You must decide: you can either not like people, or you can embrace them. You love the people who bring you happiness, but you embrace them all—even the people who provoke stress. My grandpa did that, and I try to follow his example.

My grandfather didn't need a lot. He was satisfied with a small but tidy home and the love and respect of friends and family. He worked to ensure those qualities, not to acquire stuff. In addition to his job as a custodian, he had a landscaping business. Many days he'd come home from work, change his clothes, and immediately begin tending the lawns of other folks in the neighborhood. He worked on the weekends too. My father demonstrated a similar work ethic, and I'd like to think I do as well. My grandpa rarely made more than minimum wage, but he didn't complain, and he never felt a job was beneath him. There was nobility in work and in taking care of your family. I think he believed he was a lucky man, and it would be hard to argue otherwise.

What little free time my grandfather did have was devoted to family and sports, both playing and watching the latter. A talented baseball player in high school, he had transitioned to fast-pitch softball as a young man. In the leagues around Salinas, Grandpa Danny was something of a legend; everybody talked about him. What I remember most about my grandfather was that he was a happy man. All he needed was his family, the San Francisco Giants on TV at night, and a Budweiser nearby. The two loves of his life were my grandmother and the Giants. He liked watching the 49ers too, but I think that was more about regional pride. He liked the Niners more than he liked the sport of football (although, like I said, he knew a lot about the game). Me? I've been a 49ers fan my whole life, but I knew early on that it was the *game* I truly loved, more so than the team that happened to be playing.

My father was a baseball guy as well, so I learned from them both and followed whatever sport was in season. I used to lie on the floor and watch San Francisco Giants games, with a baseball tucked under my chin, pretending I was Will Clark or Barry Bonds or Matt Williams. At an early age I figured out how to play catch with myself, using my shoulder to flip the ball into the air and catching it with my chest. Then I'd let the ball roll onto my shoulder again and repeat the act, over and over and over.

If that sounds risky, I suppose it was. I took a few pops to the head and chest, but nothing too serious. Again, I can't thank my parents enough for understanding how important that was to me and for refusing to raise me in a plastic bubble. To whatever extent was possible, they wanted me to experience the life of a little boy, and if that meant taking a baseball to the face once in a while, so be it. (Honestly, I didn't drop too many balls.)

Sometimes I'd play indoor Wiffle ball with my father. He'd set me up against the refrigerator with a small plastic bat tucked between my chin and shoulder. Then he'd throw the ball, and I'd swing away.

This was my way of gaining access to a world I couldn't otherwise enter, a world of balls and bats and gloves, of running and throwing and tackling. I spent a lot of time in my head, pretending I was an all-star quarterback or outfielder. I watched endless hours of football and baseball. And I played video games: *MLB, NBA 2K, FIFA,* and *Madden NFL.* Especially *Madden.*

I'd play alone or with friends or family, for hours at a time. I'd tuck the controller between my chin and collarbone and manipulate the buttons and joystick almost as quickly as my able-bodied competitors. Sometimes faster. I got pretty good at it. I learned how to diagram plays and sketch out a game plan through *Madden.* I learned about clock management. I learned how to use my head and to think like a coach. It wasn't the same as putting on pads and a uniform, but it was the next best thing.

* * *

My parents encouraged most of my childhood pursuits, but especially those that were related to sports. I assume they sometimes felt conflicted about this, knowing that I'd never be able to play the games that meant so much to me and wanting to spare me the pain of disappointment. If so, they never let on.

When I was growing up, my father was my best friend. In many ways our relationship was no different from that of most sons and fathers, and we bonded over sports. It brought a semblance of normalcy to our lives and was a passion we could share and enjoy. Baseball had been my father's great love. From what I heard, he was a terrific baseball player in high school, just like my grandfather had been. Dad was a catcher, which makes sense, given how tough he was. But something went awry on the path to adulthood, and a time came when he decided to live the wrong way, hang out with the wrong crowd, party too much—the kind of things that can wreck almost anyone's plans. I've been coaching high school kids long enough to have seen it happen repeatedly.

Academically and athletically, my father didn't achieve what he could have achieved. He didn't graduate from high school on time, and he didn't go on to play college baseball, which probably would have been an option for him had things turned out differently. Instead, he was sent away from home for a while and wound up getting his diploma at age nineteen, while living in Oregon. I know only the broad strokes of this period of my father's life, and I never asked for clarification. I do know that it's hard for me to reconcile the serious, industrious man who raised me with the hell-raiser he apparently once was. Life is complicated and challenging, and never more so than during adolescence. People can change, often for the better.

When my father returned from the Pacific Northwest, he went to work at a supermarket, bagging groceries. During that period, he met my mother. They married and had a baby girl, my older sister, Jackie, and my father became a self-taught carpenter and began taking classes toward a degree in respiratory therapy. By the time I came along, with an assortment of almost incomprehensible needs and issues, my dad was deep into the transition to a new career and a new life. He was twenty-four.

If I inherited my generally easygoing and accepting nature from my grandfather (and my mother), I got my determination from my father—a chip-on-the-shoulder mentality that drives me to keep moving forward, grinding and working, and doing my best to avoid the trap of self-pity. I can't imagine the pressure my father must have been under, and the awesome responsibility he assumed as a young man. He did a great job. We lived in a nice middle-class neighborhood; I had what I needed. My father did everything he could to keep us safe. I think his main priority in life was to be a provider and a protector. You might assume he wasn't around a lot because he was working so much, but that wasn't the case. No matter how tired or stressed out my dad might have been—and I imagine that was pretty much 24/7—he always made time for me. Time to play ball or watch a game or just hang out and talk. Time that made me feel like any other normal kid.

Sports had that effect on me. I enjoyed being around games. I loved the energy and the athleticism, and the obvious camaraderie.

When I was five, I attended my first hockey game. After a long absence, in 1991, the San Jose Sharks had brought the National Hockey League back to Northern California. The team played at the old Cow Palace in San Francisco for a couple of seasons before moving to a gorgeous new arena in San Jose (officially known today as the SAP Center, but colloquially referred to as—what else?—the Shark Tank). In the team's second season in San Jose, one of my great aunts got a bunch of tickets for a game. I don't know what her connection was, but somehow, she had access to great seats, lower level, right behind the glass. The whole experience mesmerized me, but the two things that stood out the most were the noise and the speed.

When you're five years old, a professional sporting event is an assault on the senses, in the best possible way. I remember yelling from the moment the puck was dropped, the way the fans cheered, and the music that played over every stoppage. Mostly, I remember the sound of bodies crashing against plexiglass, and the swish-swish of blades gliding across the ice, spraying mists of white in their wake. The players, wearing pads and helmets and skates that lifted them three inches above the rink, all looked like giants.

I knew absolutely nothing about the sport of hockey or the NHL; I'd never seen a game in person or on TV. In those days, hockey was a bit of a mystery in the Bay Area. There were no youth teams to join, no professional or college teams to cheer on. But even with no frame of reference, I became an instant fan. Each thunderous body check sent shockwaves into the stands. Just following the flight of the puck took all my focus and energy.

How did these guys even see it?!

I flinched each time the glass rattled, when two players collided, or a puck went sailing into the air and appeared to be heading right my way. But then the puck would smack into the plexiglass and fall harmlessly to the ice, and I'd laugh with relief and exhilaration. The best part? When my parents tapped me on the shoulder and pointed to the jumbotron hanging above the rink like some sort of spaceship.

"Look at that, Robert! Can you see what it says?"

I could see, all right. There on the jumbotron, in letters ten feet tall, was a personal message:

Welcome, Robert Mendez, to Your First Hockey Game!

While I was staring skyward, the crowd began to cheer. Moments later I saw someone, some . . . *thing,* rushing toward me. It was Sharkie, the team's mascot.

In reality, this was a grown man in a Sharks uniform and a plush, bulbous shark head, with jaws agape. Sharkie was supposed to be smiling, but any five-year-old could be forgiven for thinking he was about to be eaten alive. This is the risk when mascots and small children interact.

I stared in wonder as Sharkie approached my chair and held out a welcoming hand. In his palm was a souvenir hockey puck. He placed it on the tray of my wheelchair, gave me a pat on the back, and bounded away. I've been a Sharks fan ever since.

On more than one occasion in elementary school, I'd brag to my friends (and to teachers), "Guess what I'm doing tonight? I'm going to a Sharks game with my dad!" I'd talk about it all day and couldn't sit still or focus on my schoolwork. Probably drove my teachers nuts.

* * *

Part of our postgame routine was to wait around for autographs. My father was patient, and the Sharks players tended to be gracious and friendly. At Giants games, the crowds were bigger, and while the players accommodated most requests, they seemed a bit less likely to stop and interact. Not sure why, but hockey players just seemed . . . friendlier. I used to find that interesting, given how violent the sport could be.

When I was about seven or eight, my father took me to an event known as the San Jose Sharks Fan Fest. This was an annual gathering hosted by the organization to show support for fans and business members in the local community. At its heart, I suppose it was an attempt to sell more season tickets and corporate sponsorships, but to a little kid, it was a chance to meet some of the players. One of my favorite Sharks was left wing Jeff Friesen, in part because of the way he played but also because the first time I went to Fan Fest, Jeff wound up talking to me and my father for about twenty minutes. He wasn't the only one who took the time to introduce himself, but for some reason he decided to stick around and chat for a while, and he and my dad exchanged phone numbers.

That summer, Jeff came to Gilroy for the annual Garlic Festival (which is a whole lot bigger and more popular than you might imagine) and hung out with my dad and me. I thought that was pretty cool. Over the last few years, I've gotten to know a lot of professional athletes from a cross section of sports. My experience as a football coach has allowed me to meet numerous college and professional football players and coaches, but because of my experience as a wide-eyed kid at Sharks games, I'll always have a soft spot for hockey players.

To some extent, it continues to this day. A couple of years ago, I was at a game when I received a direct message (DM) on Instagram from left winger Evander Kane. This was *during* the game. Between periods, anyway.

"Hey, Coach. You have any time to meet up after the game?"

At first, I thought someone was pranking me, but it seemed like the DM might be real. I took the bait and responded.

"Yeah, absolutely," I wrote.

The response came instantly: "Great—meet me at the club level."

Worst-case scenario: my gullibility would lead to hanging out at the club level for a little while, waiting for someone who wouldn't show up, and whose identity had been appropriated by a fan with a weird sense of humor.

Best-case scenario: I'd get to say hello to one of the Sharks' better players, and then I'd be on my way.

At the club level, Evander emerged with his wife and a few teammates. We hung out and talked for half an hour. He explained that he'd read a story about me in the San Jose *Mercury News*, and that he wanted to introduce himself.

That was one of the first times I realized the effect I could have on people—not because I'd done anything special but because of my existence. Because I went about my business every day, despite challenges and obstacles that others might find incomprehensible.

To me, it was just life. To others it was . . . I don't know. Inspiring, I guess. At the time I didn't think about it much. A few more years would pass before I'd embrace the role that others had thrust upon me: that of being an inspirational person.

That night, on the club level of the SAP Center, I merely was giddy with excitement because I was hanging out with one of my favorite players.

Fast-forward a few years, and I'm not only hanging out in the locker room or at practice with some of these guys, but I'm playing PlayStation 4 online with them as well, which might be even cooler!

It's all a little surreal. I didn't get into coaching to meet professional athletes or other celebrities. I didn't do it to spread a message or be a poster child for overcoming adversity. Never in my wildest dreams did I anticipate notoriety of any kind, as that wasn't important to me. I wanted to be a coach because football became my passion. I loved sports more than anything, and I believed that somehow, maybe, they could provide an avenue to a meaningful life.

I had no idea how I would get there. I figured that if I was doing what I loved, things would work out.

CHAPTER THREE

onfidence has rarely been much of an issue for me. I'm not sure exactly why. Good DNA, perhaps—you draw the proverbial short straw in one sense, and God compensates by giving you the long straw in another. Again, it probably also has something to do with the way I was raised, in an atmosphere of love and support, but one in which I wasn't treated delicately or even differently.

I was encouraged to push boundaries and to embrace a spirit of adventure. When I'd lie on the floor and play catch by myself, my parents didn't stand by and fret over whether I'd drop the ball on my face. They knew it would happen and that I would recover. Bumps and bruises are part of growing up, and while my parents had more to worry about than most, they didn't let their anxiety impede my progress. They wanted me to be as normal as possible, and that meant discouraging any tendency toward defeatism.

One day I came home from middle school and told my father that my friend Alex was going to try out for the school soccer team. I wasn't upset or envious. I was happy for Alex and curious to see how he would do. We had played a lot of pickup and rec soccer together. Alex was always the best player on the field, and as one of the goalies on his team, I hardly ever got any action because the ball rarely made it over midfield.

"Alex is going to do great, huh, Dad?"

My father paused. Then he tried to steer the conversation in a particular direction—one in which the focus would be on what I *could* do, as opposed to what I *could not* do.

"It's okay, Robert," he began. "You're going to have your own adventure. You'll see."

I laughed. "No, Dad. It's fine. I'm happy for Alex."

My dad nodded, smiled a little. He was relieved to have misread the situation, but I don't think he wanted to let on.

It had to have been hard for my parents, to have this vision of what it would be like to raise a healthy, rambunctious little boy and then suddenly discover that his life would be filled with extraordinary challenges. My father responded to this not with fear or trepidation (not that I saw, anyway, although I'm sure he felt it) but by forever pushing me and by pushing those around me. I imagine that the natural inclination of any parent of a child born with physical challenges would be to go overboard on the protection. No one coddled me, however. I never doubted that I was loved, deeply and profoundly, but the default response from my parents, especially my father, was to encourage experimentation and risk, to soak up life's pains and joys.

Kids get hurt all the time, physically and emotionally. But they also succeed. They grow and learn and find their way in the world. I would be no different. Yes, I needed help getting dressed in the morning. I needed an aide at school to assist with feeding and bathroom breaks, and the other mundane tasks of daily life that most people take for granted. Yet these quickly became second nature to me, so I was, for the most part, like any other kid.   •

As a toddler, I learned by trial and error to navigate my own little corner of the universe. In the same way that other kids learn to walk by wobbling from one room to another and crashing into end tables or falling on their faces, I learned to roll or bounce across the living room. It was all I knew, and I responded organically. I understood that I couldn't do certain things, but these things didn't define me, and I didn't consider them shortcomings. They were simply part of my existence.

I have few memories of my parents wringing their hands over the possibility that some terrible fate might befall me the moment I went outside to play or to school. More often, it was the school district throwing up yellow caution tape, no doubt for liability reasons. My parents, especially my father, were relentless about advocating on my behalf; they aggressively pursued outlets for access and opportunity. For example, I had an Individualized Educational Plan (IEP) at school, common for any student with a documented disability recognized under the law. An IEP stipulates that the student, due to the nature of his disability, is entitled to certain unique services and instruction.

An IEP is typically associated with students who have a documented learning disability, such as attention deficit disorder or dyslexia. I had no such label, but because of my physical challenges, at school I sometimes needed an aide's help. I could get around fine in my motorized wheelchair, and I could write essays and answer test questions using a pen clenched between my teeth. Even so, some tasks faced in the course of an ordinary school day required assistance, like taking out my books and getting set up for class. The IEP ensured that I would have the same opportunities as other students, even if some concessions or modifications were required. This was a good thing, as it greatly helped me be part of a mainstream school experience.

Sometimes problems did occur. My parents insisted that the IEP not be used as an excuse for me to get out of work, or for a teacher to avoid the admittedly cumbersome task of making sure I was involved. For example, it was easier to give me a pass on a biology lab than to let me be part of it, in whatever way I could. When I was in middle school, I specifically remember my parents kicking up a big storm over this. It was a hands-on lab, clinical work followed by a written report documenting the lab's outcome. Standard stuff for most kids. I was told I didn't have to do it. I wouldn't be punished in any way, and my grade wouldn't suffer. But I also wouldn't have the learning experience (not to mention the fun) of taking part in the lab.

My parents went straight to the school.

"What's wrong with you guys?" my father said. "Robert has the ability to organize and learn. He can make a contribution. Let him be a part of the lab."

Everything worked out in the end, and I actually felt bad for the teacher. She was young and inexperienced, and I have no doubt that she meant no harm. Managing a middle school classroom is challenging under the best circumstances; my presence made it even more difficult. She may have been worried about my safety, or the safety of others if they lost focus for some reason. But denying access, even for benign reasons, isn't right, and that's why I was fortunate to have not only a solid IEP but also righteous parents. Some kids get embarrassed if their parents interfere with anything that transpires at school; I was proud of my parents for sticking up for me. I always knew they had my back, and that knowledge helped give me the confidence I needed to fit in like any other kid, academically, athletically, and socially.

* * *

I was in eighth grade the first time I remember saying the words that have become the rallying cry of the kids I coach and my motto for life—the words that also appear on the cover of this memoir. It happened at a dance at Brownell Middle School in Gilroy. I was hanging out with some of my friends at the edge of the gym floor, listening to a DJ spin through a playlist dominated by Britney Spears and the Backstreet Boys. As often happens in middle school, most of the kids on the floor were girls, fearlessly dancing either alone or in pairs or in small groups, while packs of thirteen-year-old boys cowered on the sidelines, terrified of busting a pathetic move in front of everyone, and especially of being rejected.

There was Cece, the prettiest girl in eighth grade, waiting for someone to get up the nerve to approach her. I knew Cece a little from school, and like everyone else, I had a big crush on her. I figured this was as good a time as any to let her know how I felt.

"Next slow song that comes on, I'm going to go ask her to dance," I said to my friends. They looked at me like I was crazy.

"Dude, you can't do that."

I laughed. "Really, bro? Who says I can't?"

Moments later, when the tempo slowed, I leaned back into one of the touch pads on the headrest of my chair (there are two, which act as gas pedal and steering wheel) and made a beeline for Cece. At first, I didn't say anything. I just drove a couple of big circles around her, then did a tight doughnut or two for added effect.

"What's up?" I said.

She laughed, which was good. She could have run away in terror.

"Want to dance?" I asked.

"Okay. But . . ."

I nodded. "Just put your arms around my shoulders."

She smiled, and for the next three and a half minutes, we slow danced to Britney. When the song ended, we talked. And then we talked some more. And then we danced some more. The following Monday, when I saw Cece in school, I was more nervous than I had been at the dance. I wondered if she would pretend that nothing had happened. I was prepared to have my heart stomped on. Instead, we talked some more. We began spending time together, and for the next three years, Cece and I were a couple.

WHO SAYS I CAN'T?

Who says I can't?

That became my thing, though mostly in my mind. I'd say it to myself whenever someone told me I couldn't do something or placed an artificial and arbitrary roadblock in my path. But sometimes I'd actually shout it out loud, like after smoking someone in *Madden* or, much later, while playing beer pong at a party. Yes, I did go to parties. I was a fairly typical high school kid, which meant I did reasonably well academically, had some good friends, tried to balance work with play and stay out of trouble. But I wasn't perfect. Far from it.

My mother and grandmother relentlessly stressed the importance of being kind and considerate. They understood that people make mistakes, especially kids and young adults, so they had compassion for the inevitable screwups that mark a typical adolescence.

"But if you make a mistake," my grandmother used to say, "don't let it be the kind of mistake that affects other people. Don't hurt anyone."

I used to think about that a lot. I still do. Those are wise words, made even wiser by the subtext, which is that anytime you mess up, it probably affects *someone*. None of us exists in a vacuum. When we realize that everything we do, every action large and small, has some sort of ripple effect, it helps to keep the moral compass in good working order.

Then again, kids are kids, and boys will be boys.

46

• • •

I was twelve years old the first time I got involved in a disagreement that had the potential to escalate into something more dramatic and potentially dangerous. It's interesting the way friendships develop and the extent to which a child's personality and worldview can be shaped not just by family but by the neighborhood in which he or she is raised. In most suburban areas, your first friends are the kids who live nearby. You become introduced to one another on the cul-de-sac, you have playdates at one another's houses, and then you attend the same elementary school, the same middle school, and probably the same high school. Relationships and identities are forged early, and for parents, a bit of luck is involved. They hope the neighbor's kid is a good influence, raised by parents with similar values. If so, their job is easier, and there are fewer sleepless nights.

I was fortunate. My neighborhood boasted an abundance of nice kids from solid families. There were block parties and backyard barbecues and an open-door policy among friends: my house is your house, and your house is mine. We bonded early, and we took care of one another. We played kickball and soccer and Wiffle ball. I was treated like any other kid. There were things I couldn't do, but I never was excluded. In kickball, for example, someone else might kick the ball for me, but I'd run the bases in my wheel-chair. This was as natural as could be and contributed greatly to my feeling like one of the guys. We were all reasonably decent students, and while we weren't ex-actly angels, neither were we interested in creating trouble for anyone.

But it's strange how the same general area, with families from strikingly similar socioeconomic back-grounds, can produce pockets of delinquency and nastiness. So much of it seems random and uncon-trollable.

Another group of kids, roughly the same age as we were, lived nearby, maybe a half dozen blocks away. We all attended the same elementary school but rarely hung out together outside of school. When we did see them, the interactions were usually unpleas-ant. These kids were more likely to get into trouble in school. They were the kids who started smoking ciga-rettes and weed in middle school. They got into fights. They welcomed bullies into their midst. They were the first kids I knew who figured out how to ac-cess pornography on the internet.

Now, I understand that a lot of this stuff is un-healthy, though not entirely uncommon during ado-lescence. But this particular group of boys accelerated the process to an unnerving extent, in part because a few of them happened to have older brothers, whose gravitational pull, for better or worse, was undeniable. In my eyes, they were the bad kids, and we were the good kids. A simplification, perhaps, but generally accurate in my memory. My parents put few restrictions on my movement or activity, as long as I was hanging out with the kids on our cul-de-sac. But if they'd known the sphere of influence had been expanded to include the boys from a few blocks away, they wouldn't have been happy. It was a simple rule, and I adhered to it.

Most of the time.

When my group of friends did cross paths with the other group, it was usually in school and unavoidable. On occasion, my buddies and I would wander away and find ourselves in enemy territory, so to speak. Or the other kids would venture into our neighborhood. In either case, we'd get into it a little bit, toss out insults and threats, then go our separate ways. But on one memorable occasion the confrontation turned physical. Insults led to pushing and shoving, which eventually led to wrestling and punches being thrown. You might think that middle school boys can't do a lot of damage, and you'd probably be right. But when you're in the thick of something like this, it can feel like a riot, especially from a wheelchair.

For a few moments, I just sat there, transfixed. I wouldn't say I was scared, exactly. I felt the rush of adrenaline that anyone would feel in the middle of a brawl, but also the frustration and uncertainty that came with being physically incapable of joining the fray or defending my friends. If I may state the obvious, having no arms or legs is a huge disadvantage in a street fight. I knew it. My buddies knew it. Even the "bad kids" knew it. So I was left alone. A spectator relegated to the sideline of my own life.

Or not.

As the action swirled about me, I watched with growing agitation. I saw one of the bigger kids throwing punches and grappling with my buddy Abed, who appeared to be in trouble. Anger rose in my throat, and I could feel my arm throwing phantom punches (yes, that happens—more on that later). Suddenly, I was guiding my chair across the blacktop, bearing down on the boy who was hurting my friend. Faster, faster, faster, like a driver in a demolition derby.

Thump!

My chair hit him in the legs and sent him staggering backward. I heard him grunt and curse, saw him stumble to the ground. Now free, Abed looked at me with amazement and smiled.

"Dude, that was awesome!"

And it was. For a moment.

The other kid quickly caught his breath and scrambled to his feet. Without hesitation he charged at me. I braced myself. For what, I'm not sure. Maybe he'd knock me over. Maybe he'd punch me in the face. Either way, I could do nothing. Maybe I had it coming.

He stopped, inches from my chair, his face contorted and aflame with rage, his hands balled into fists. What could he do? No one hits a kid in a wheelchair, right? Not even if the kid in the wheelchair delivered the first blow. He was in a no-win situation: fiercely pissed off, and rightfully so, but handcuffed by the obvious immorality of striking a defenseless person. Except, again, I had hit him first.

The three of us stood motionless for a few seconds, until the kid figured it out. He took a deep breath, coughed up a bunch of mucous, and spat it directly in my face. I winced as he cursed me out again. Then I cursed right back at him. Abed jumped in between us and shoved the kid away. That's when we realized everyone else was staring at us. My friends all rallied around to see if I was okay. There was more pushing and shoving, more threats leveled in both directions, but it also was clear that everyone realized a line had been crossed. Or nearly crossed. And with that realization came a quick de-escalation. We went one way; they went the other.

As we walked home, soiled and sweaty, Abed threw an arm around my shoulder.

"Rob, you're crazy, man."

I laughed. He had a point. I could have been badly hurt. As an adult, and especially as someone who coaches young men, I don't condone violence. I condone empathy, compassion, and love. But as a twelve-year-old kid determined to find a place in the world, unrestrained by his physical limitations?

I've gotta admit—it felt pretty good.

CHAPTER FOUR

The transition from middle school to high school can be difficult for anyone, and it wasn't easy for me.

Throughout middle school I had traveled to and from school with the same reliable group of friends, but with high school came abundant opportunities and diverging interests. Specifically, I'm referring to organized sports. Whether through video games or pickup ball in the neighborhood, or through my uncle's involvement in Little League baseball, I had always found some way to satisfy my desire to have a role in the games that young men and young women naturally play.

But high school sports are different. They are, by definition and design, less inclusive and more competitive. The games are taken more seriously. There are tryouts for teams at every level, and inevitably, some aspirants are cut out of the system. For me, there was no tryout, no opportunity to be part of the program. I didn't feel sorry for myself, but I did notice a subtle shift in what this would mean to my life. I loved sports, and with each passing year, I wanted more than ever to be involved.

On the first day of school, when the final bell rang, I headed for the exit, as I always did, while most of my friends went to the locker room to get ready for football practice. I had no one I could walk home with. Moreover, I didn't really want to go home. I wanted to go to football practice! So I waited for my friends to change and then joined them on the long walk to a distant field, where the freshman team was about to begin its first practice. They looked cool and confident in their uniforms, their cleats clacking on the pavement and their helmets dangling from their hands.

They looked like young warriors, and I wanted nothing more than to be on the battlefield with them.

"You going home?" one of them asked as we approached the field.

I shrugged. "Maybe I'll watch for a while."

The freshman team practiced on the outfield of the junior varsity baseball field. I pulled my chair up near the dugout, roughly a hundred yards from the practice field, and watched as Abed disappeared into a pack of boys. At that time, I was probably more of a baseball or hockey fan than I was a football fan. I'd never been to a football game in person, but I'd been to dozens of Sharks and Giants games. I'd been on a Little League team, and I'd grown up in a family that worshipped at the altar of baseball. But that day, as I watched my friends playing football, and apparently having a great time, things began to change.

Part of the reason was social. I was an extremely outgoing kid, and I loved hanging out with my buddies. Now, for the first time, they were part of a club I couldn't access. It wasn't their fault. It was just the way things were. How could I possibly play football? What could I offer?

But even from that distance, I could tell that I understood better than some of the boys on the field what was required to play the game. This brings us to something I mentioned earlier: the idea that a person born without arms or legs has no idea what it would be like to throw a football or swing a baseball bat. On a purely factual and physical level, that's entirely true. Even so, the mind and body are wondrous mechanisms, connected in ways that might not be obvious.

While I've never experienced the act of throwing a football and never have felt the tactile sensation of leather against fingers, I can imagine precisely what it would be like. I don't mean in some fantastic way, like imagining what it would be like to fly without wings. I'm talking about something very specific. You've probably heard of phantom pain—the sensation of a severed limb sending signals to the brain long after it has been separated from the body. In my case, active nerves in my shoulders and lower buttocks communicate with my brain, and the resulting conversation can be surprisingly lively. I don't have an arm, but I can feel it rearing back behind my head and then slinging a ball thirty yards down the field in a tight spiral. I can move my chair back and forth on a basketball court and feel as though my legs are doing the work. And I can see myself executing a perfect crossover dribble as my defender stumbles and falls.

I can feel it in my arms, hands, legs. Maybe not in the same exact way you would feel it, as an able-bodied person, but I do feel it.

So there I was that afternoon, after my first day at Gilroy High School, watching from a distance and moving my shoulders back and forth, pretending to throw the ball, feeling it snap off my hand. I watched certain kids, and I could tell right away which of them were athletes, and which of them were not, by evaluating their footwork or mechanics. I understood what it meant to be an athlete, and I knew in my head and my heart that if I could get out there, if I had been born with arms and legs, I would have been an asset.

Because I was a competitor, and because I understood what the coaches were trying to convey.

But none of that mattered. All I could do was watch.

After practice I walked home with Abed and a couple of the other guys. I told my parents I had been at practice and that it looked like a lot of fun. They didn't make a big deal out of it. They knew better than to fuel whatever frustration or sadness I might be feeling. And it wasn't like I was crushed by the experience. But I did feel like I was missing out on something, and I wondered how I would fill the void.

The next day I went to practice again. I parked my chair in the exact same spot and watched for a couple of hours as my friends played football. This time I really watched closely. This was 2002, so there were no smartphones to provide distraction. Wherever you were, you were there, and you typically were compelled to engage on some level.

I sat in my wheelchair, with two hours to kill until practice was over and I could go home with my friends. It wasn't quite like watching the 49ers on television or even like playing *Madden*, but it was football, and I was closer to it than I had ever been.

Since this was still early in the season, practices consisted primarily of position drills; they hadn't dived heavily into the playbook yet. I took an immediate interest in the quarterback drills, in part because one of my friends, Chris, was a quarterback, but also because quarterback was the glamour position. The quarterback was like the coach on the field, the guy who got all the attention in televised games, and the player who seemed to control all the action in *Madden*.

I was too far away to clearly hear what was going on. I could tell the coaches were shouting a lot but couldn't understand what they were saying. I decided to focus on the players' footwork and delivery. The boys would alternate taking a snap from center, and then they would drop back quickly.

As they did that, I could finally make out one of the coaches shouting, "One-two-plant-throw!"

I then understood the drill: two steps back, plant hard, and throw the ball. It was all about repetition. Muscle memory. But it was also about understanding which foot to lead with: if you're right handed, your first step back should be your right foot. And it was fascinating, because I got it! I understood exactly what the coach was trying to convey, even if some of the players didn't. Chris was one of the guys who had some trouble with the drill. The next day in school, I gave him a few suggestions to make the drill easier, and while I wouldn't have blamed him for questioning the source, he appreciated the input.

"Okay," he said. "I'll try it today."

The third day was the same thing. My friends went to practice, and I watched from the dugout.

This was the routine, and I was okay with it. But as practice ended that day, and the players gathered together, I noticed a couple of the coaches talking and looking in my direction. A couple of my friends nodded, pointed. Then one of the coaches began waving at me. Another coach began waving, as did several of the players.

"Rob!" they yelled. "Come on over!"

It had been raining on and off all day, so the ground was wet and soft. Rather than taking a loner route across concrete, I rolled straight for the coaches, and a couple of times my wheels began to spin. I had no idea why I was being summoned, but I felt a rush of excitement, and in my haste, I nearly got my chair stuck in the mud.

As the post-practice meeting continued, a couple of the coaches pulled me aside. The defensive coordinator, Skip Bloom, did most of the talking.

"You're Robert, right?"

"Yes, sir."

"You have a bunch of friends on the team?"

I smiled and began saying their names. "Yeah. Abed, Nick, Justin . . ."

Coach Bloom nodded.

"Would you like a jersey?"

"A jersey?" I repeated, incredulously.

"Yeah. We'd like you to be part of the team in any way that you can. What do you say?"

I felt a little bit choked up. I could scarcely believe what was happening.

"Yes, Coach. I would love that."

"All right, then—let's go inside and find you a jersey."

I followed them into the high school and into the locker room. Most of the kids on the team were pretty low key—that's just the way boys are—but I remember a couple of my friends smiling and nodding as we walked away. Inside, the coaches took me into the equipment room, where a half-empty box of jerseys was waiting. Coach Bloom rummaged through the box.

"We don't have a lot left. Would you like a high number or a low number?"

It didn't matter, but since they asked . . .

"Low would be cool," I said. "I mean—I'm usually number one."

I laughed. Coach Bloom kind of rolled his eyes a bit and pulled out a jersey.

"How about number twelve?"

"Sure, Coach. Twelve would be great." (And it was. As my girlfriend would later say when she saw the jersey, "Hey, it's perfect. Your favorite number is one, and mine is two. That's twelve!")

Coach Bloom walked over and put the jersey in my lap. It was badly wrinkled and musty. It also was just about the most beautiful thing I'd ever seen.

"Thank you, Coach."

"You're welcome. See you tomorrow."

The next day in school, one of the coaches, who also happened to teach one of my classes, pulled me aside.

"Hey, Mendez," he said. Right away I could feel my chest puffing out, swelling with pride. You see, the football coaches tended to call the players by their surnames. It was simultaneously a display of gruffness and respect. In school, I'd always been "Robert" or "Rob." Now I was "Mendez." I was one of the guys.

"Yes, Coach?"

"We're on the road tomorrow. You want to join us?"

I was speechless. I'd been invited to join the team less than one day earlier, and already I was being offered a chance to travel with the team to its season opener, on a Friday night at Terra Nova High School, located nearly eighty miles away in Pacifica.

"Oh my God," I stammered. "Of course, Coach. I'd love that."

He nodded. "All right. We just have to clear it with your parents."

I went to practice that day, wearing my freshly laundered Gilroy jersey with number twelve on the front and back. There wasn't a lot for me to do, but I enjoyed being part of it—being close enough to talk with my friends between drills and to cheer everyone on. I liked that every practice seemed so organized and had so much attention to detail. Each coach and player had a job to do. There was almost no standing around, the way there was at baseball practice. It was so *busy*.

After practice I left with my buddies, eager to get home and ask my parents if I could travel with the team to Pacifica the next day.

"Mom, Dad!" I shouted when I entered the house. "You won't believe it."

"You're traveling with the team?" my father said, rather perfunctorily.

"Yeah. How did you know?"

My mom laughed. "We got a call from school this afternoon. They needed our permission."

"What did you say?"

My father looked at me like it was the stupidest question he'd ever heard.

"Have fun," he said.

"All right!" I shouted. Then I challenged him to a game of *Madden*.

* * *

Terra Nova was a nonleague game and easily the most distant opponent we'd face all season. An eighty-mile trip on clogged Bay Area freeways can easily take three hours, so it also was the only game for which we traveled by charter bus. Two buses carried all three teams: freshman, junior varsity, varsity. I took a window seat; Chris, the quarterback, took the aisle. I was so excited I could barely sit still, and I found myself talking Chris's ear off. He didn't say a lot in response, and after a while I noticed he was sweating like crazy, even though the air-conditioning on the bus had been cranked.

"Hey, man. You okay?"

Chris turned to me and tried to smile. His eyes were wide.

"Don't worry. You're going do great."

He nodded subtly but didn't say anything.

This was my introduction to the intensity of organized football, and it was like nothing I'd ever experienced. Baseball was so relaxed. Even on game days, no one got nervous or worked up. You could go through batting practice or fielding drills without breaking a sweat, while chatting or joking around with your buddies the whole time. And once the game started, what was the worst that could happen? You might get hit by a pitch, which would sting a little, or you could suffer the indignity of striking out or dropping a fly ball.

But football?

This was different. It was serious, scary business, even for a bunch of ninth graders. There was precious little clowning around on the bus, and even less in the locker room as we prepared to take the field. The coaches gave their pregame talks, which started out quiet and instructional and gradually escalated to fist-pumping fury as we all gathered in a circle and let out a battle cry. Then we ran out onto the field. At the time I didn't fully comprehend what was happening, but it didn't take long to catch on. Football is a violent game, even when played by fourteen-year-olds. Helmets and pads notwithstanding, it hurts to get hit. The anxiety and nervousness that permeate a locker room in the moments before kickoff stems from the players' inherent and perfectly reasonable fear of the unknown.

Will I get hurt?

Will I be courageous or cowardly?

Will I let myself down? Will I let my friends and coaches down?

As with any sport, there's always trepidation over the possibility of publicly screwing up—forgetting the plays or missing an assignment and getting chewed out by the coaches as a result—but fundamentally, football is about toughness in the face of adversity. That's one of things I like about it: that it reflects so much of life (my own life in particular). How will you respond when you get knocked down? Because you *will* get knocked down. It's not a question of *if*; it's a question of *when*. And *how often.*

You can't control when or how the blows will be delivered. You can only control your preparedness and your response.

That's football.

That's life.

Thanks to the thoughtfulness of my coaches and teammates, I had a few duties that day and on game days (or nights) throughout the season. For example, I carried a spare football and a kicking tee in an equipment bag that hung from the back of my chair. When it was time for our team to kick off, I'd drive my wheelchair onto the field, and the kicker would remove the tee from the bag. Or I'd give the ball and kicking block to whoever was assigned to hold the ball on extra-point attempts. Then I'd drive off the field and join my teammates on the sideline, close enough to the action that I could hear every grunt and groan; close enough that I could call to my friends by name, and they'd know it was me; close enough to give them a fist bump with my shoulder when they came off the field. And close enough that sometimes the coaches had to tell me to back off, because I was either in the way or creeping onto the playing field, which was not only against the rules . . . but dangerous.

"Easy there, Mendez. Stay behind the line."

"Oh . . . sorry, Coach."

I don't remember the final score of that game, but we lost. Terra Nova was a smaller school than Gilroy but had a more prominent and successful football program, and the whole point of playing them was to test ourselves in advance of the conference schedule.

We played well enough that nobody seemed terribly disappointed afterward.

I was just happy to be part of the program and to play some small role on the freshman team. I was grateful to spend time with my friends and to have a place on the sideline on game days. Though perhaps I should amend that statement. You see, I was on the sideline only for road games. When Gilroy played at home, I was the public address announcer.

When I was a little kid, watching sports on television or playing games with my father, I often pretended I was the public address announcer or one of the broadcasters. I can vividly remember how it started. When I'd go to Sharks games with my dad, one of my favorite parts of the game was right after a goal was scored, and the crowd would go crazy. Then there'd be a brief moment of quiet, as everyone waited for the PA announcer to tell us what we already knew: the name of the person who had just scored the goal (along with the names of those who had assisted, which we didn't know, because following first and second assists in hockey can be almost impossible without instant replay).

Sometimes my father would repeat what the PA announcer had said, in a big, booming voice, which always made me laugh. Then he'd pat me on the back.

"You could do that someday, Robert. You could announce games."

After a while I started doing it too. As soon as the puck hit the net, I'd scream at the top of my lungs: "San Jose Sharks goal by number thirty-nine, Jeff Friesen, at 5:55 of the second period!"

I started doing this at home, as well. I tried to beat the announcer on TV. And then I began listening carefully to the broadcasters, as well as the PA announcers. I understood the different roles they played—how one announcer would describe the action on the ice, while the other announcer (often an ex-player) would contribute analysis and more flavorful description or stories. The interplay between the two was critical to creating an optimum broadcasting experience. It was like a dance, with the play-by-play man pausing briefly to allow the color commentator to jump in and provide insight from an athletic perspective.

When I watched a Sharks game, sometimes I'd turn down the volume and play both parts myself. After a while, I got pretty good at it. Then I started doing the same thing for the Giants and 49ers, and for the Golden State Warriors. Sometimes I pretended I was in the booth, addressing a television audience. Other times I pretended I was a courtside PA announcer.

My family would tell you I was never exactly camera shy, and the endless videos of me hamming it up at family gatherings would support that notion. I didn't mind when one of my aunts recorded my broadcast performances. At first, I watched the videos because it was cool to see myself onscreen, acting like a real broadcaster, but after a while, I began studying the videos, trying to learn from my mistakes. Somewhere along the line, I began to dream about being a professional broadcaster. I loved sports, and while it wasn't realistic to think that I'd ever play competitively at the high school level (to say nothing of the professional level), there was no reason I couldn't pursue a career as a broadcaster, based on the job qualifications:

Knowledge of the game? *Check!*

Love of the game? *Check!*

Facility with the language? *Check!*

Strong work ethic? *Check!*

An ability to overcome innate shyness? *Check!*

Many things in my life were out of reach: always had been out of reach and always would be. Not broadcasting. I could do this. And I could be good at it.

At Brownell Middle School, I took the first tenuous steps toward making that dream become a reality. I still don't know exactly how it happened, but I'm pretty sure my father played a role by letting one of my school counselors know I loved sports and that I spent a lot of time in front of the TV, pretending I was a broadcaster. My parents constantly strove to help me be involved, to feel a sense of normalcy and inclusion, and I don't doubt that this was another occasion when their advocacy played a significant role.

Regardless, in seventh grade I became the PA announcer for the Brownell Middle School basketball team. I didn't get a lot of coaching on how to do the job, but it wasn't that complicated. I sat courtside, next to the scorekeeper, and announced to the meager crowd of family and friends the pertinent facts: starting lineups, the names of players entering and leaving the game, time outs. The beauty of being a PA announcer at this level is that I had the freedom to go off script. I could announce the names of players who scored or who made a particularly strong play on defense. I could become animated:

"Alvarez swats that ball into the cheap seats!"

I could be more than a boring PA—I could be a color commentator and play-by-play announcer as well. I loved it.

It helped that I received positive feedback. One day, in the spring of eighth grade, I was in the locker room with my aide, getting changed for swimming class, when I was approached by one of the physical education teachers, Jeff Ross. Coach Ross was a well-liked teacher and swimming coach in Gilroy. He was an extremely high-energy guy, and today that energy was on full display.

"Robert!" he bellowed. "I've got the perfect job for you!"

"What is it, Coach?" I said, feigning indifference. "You guys are always asking me to do stuff." This was true. It was also true that I didn't mind.

"All right," he said, getting right in my face. "Hear me out." I laughed. You couldn't help but hear Coach Ross, and you couldn't help but admire his enthusiasm. "I don't know if you're aware of this, but I do the PA announcing for the Gavilan College football games."

Gavilan is a community college in Gilroy. I knew they had a football team. I did not know that Coach Ross was their PA announcer.

"Okay," I said.

"Well, they lost their baseball announcer, so they're looking for a replacement. I thought of you right away." He took a step back, gave me a big smile. "Come on, Robert. What do you say?"

"Sure, Coach. Why not?"

Coach Ross clapped his hands. "Awesome! I'll get back to you with the details."

That spring I worked at least a dozen home games for the Gavilan College baseball team, which left me with a decent PA/broadcasting résumé for a kid not even out of middle school. A few months later, when the Gilroy High School football team played at home, I was the PA announcer. This was a new role not just for me but also for the program. Previously, there had been announcers only for the JV and varsity games.

The freshman game, which was either the first of the Friday triple-header or played on a different day, was contested in comparative silence. There were no starting lineups, no one to shout, "First down, *Gilroy!*" or anything like that.

Although it was a hole in the program likely noticed only by the players and their families, it was a hole nonetheless. Shortly before the first home game, that hole was plugged when Coach Bloom asked me if I'd be interested in being the PA announcer for the freshman games. Coach Bloom's invitation meant a lot to me because his father had been the longtime announcer for Gilroy's varsity football games. It was like being invited into some type of fraternity. I had already announced basketball games and baseball games, so why not football? If I had any reluctance, it was because I wouldn't get to be on the sidelines with my teammates for home games. But I liked being the PA announcer too.

I may not have been an athlete, but the athlete's world was opening up.

CHAPTER FIVE

CHAPTER FIVE

When an opportunity presents itself, you should be eager to seize it. That means not only recognizing the opportunity for what it is but also being willing to risk failure or embarrassment or any number of other negative outcomes.

The summer before my junior year in high school, I became a fixture at preseason varsity football practices. I didn't anticipate that my role would be any greater than it had been the previous two seasons. Most of my friends had been elevated to the varsity team, and I was grateful to be a small part of the program. Like the players, I became more familiar with the drills and routines, and more confident in my knowledge of how they were supposed to be executed. One of the defining characteristics of a strong program is consistency across all levels: teams run the same drills and offensive sets at the freshman level as they do at the varsity level. By the time a player has been in the program for a few years, he can communicate with his teammates and coaches in shorthand. Everyone speaks the same language, and less time is devoted to introducing concepts than to mastering them.

At practice, I was primarily a spectator, but I was highly inquisitive and studious. Some days I felt like a sponge, soaking up the coach-player interplay and focusing on the nuances of various drills from a perspective that, frankly, the players themselves didn't have. I spent a lot of time with the quarterbacks, because a couple of them were my friends and I was fascinated with the position and how much responsibility was heaped on the quarterback's shoulders. At every level of football, from high school to the NFL, the quarterback tends to be the most recognizable player on the field. And with good reason—every play goes through his hands.

Football practices are beehives of activity, with different groups completing different drills in different areas of the field. Our offensive coordinator, Coach Tim Pierleoni, would move from one drill to another, stopping briefly at each station to monitor the progress of the quarterbacks, receivers, running backs, and offensive linemen. Our defensive coordinator would do the same with defensive backs, linebackers, and defensive linemen. Various assistant coaches would oversee the individual drills, but sometimes there weren't enough coaches to go around.

One day, as practice started, Coach Pierleoni stepped away from the quarterbacks to check on another group. Most of the guys had been around for a while and knew the routine, so the expectation was that they'd figure out how to get started on their own, and by the time Coach Pierleoni returned, the drill would be in full swing. But kids are kids, and sometimes it's more fun to stand around and shoot the breeze. After this had gone on for a few minutes, I spotted an opening. I don't know what made me do it, but suddenly I heard myself yelling:

"Okay, guys. Let's get this thing going!"

Even though I was in a wheelchair and had never played a minute of football, I wasn't exactly an outsider. We were friends. We liked and respected one another. Even so, I wasn't a player, and even if I had been, it might not have made any difference. The occasional senior captain notwithstanding, players don't order one another around. That's a coach's role. But I was motivated by a desire to get involved, to see if I had something more to offer. As everyone looked at me, some with smiles, some with what can best be described as bewilderment, I barked again.

"Velasco, Tovar," I said, addressing two of my friends. "Which one of you is going to start over Peter this year?"

They both laughed. Peter, who had the inside track on the job, did not laugh.

"Shut your mouth, Mendez!" he said. But I could tell he wasn't really angry.

"Come on, guys," I repeated. "Let's get to work before Coach P comes back."

With that, the drill commenced, and I was in charge. It was a footwork drill I'd watched Coach Pierleoni direct at least a hundred times. If you're a casual football observer, you'll be forgiven for thinking that arm strength is all that matters to a quarterback. The best quarterbacks can throw a rope, for sure, but they also have field vision, intelligence, and footwork. The latter of these is crucial, as you never want a quarterback to be motionless in the pocket while trying to find a receiver. For one thing, an immobile quarterback is easy to sack; for another, he's more likely to get hurt when he's tackled.

So the quarterbacks worked incessantly on footwork. During this particular drill, Coach P would stand in front of the quarterback and yell, "Go!" The quarterback would drop back quickly and then hold the ball high, cocked and ready to throw, while tiptoeing in place. At the same time, Coach P would hold up one, two, or three fingers. The quarterback had to yell out the number of fingers being held up, while continuing to move his feet as fast as possible and holding the ball high and back, ready to be delivered. Coach P would keep changing the number, over and over, until the player was basically exhausted.

Some guys didn't understand the point of the drill, but I did, because I'd been exposed to similar exercises throughout my life. As I mentioned before, I was only eighteen months old when I was assigned an adaptive physical education teacher from the Gilroy School District. His name was Pete Pedroza, and he was one of the most important people in my life from about age one until I was fifteen, when I entered high school and we stopped working together. Coach Pete was inventive, compassionate, and endlessly upbeat; he is without question one of the most positive influences on my life, and one of the main reasons I have always had an open mind about new experiences and challenges. As far back as I can remember, he tried to think of new ways for me to work out and push myself. I don't recall him ever getting frustrated or angry.

When I was no more than five or six, we started doing an exercise in which Pete would have me lie on the ground. Then he would stand over me and drop an inflated balloon. My job was to prevent the balloon from touching the ground, either by blowing air toward it, or by moving my body and blocking its fall, and then somehow pushing it back into the air. If the drill continued long enough, it could become not just intense but exhausting. And to make it even more challenging, Coach Pete would hold up one or more fingers and instruct me to shout out the corresponding number while continuing to keep the balloon airborne. The point of the exercise was to become acclimated to multitasking—to promote mental acuity even while under physical duress. Of course, to a five-year-old it was just a game. But looking back, I can see how valuable it was to my development and to helping me adapt to the challenges I would face later in life, rather than defaulting to helplessness.

I know full well the power of the mind. Just as surely as a positive mindset can propel you to heights and accomplishments you never thought possible, a negative attitude can lead to a deterioration in the quality of your life. Hey, I've had bad days, believe me. I know how it feels to wake up with a gray cloud over your head and to wonder how you can get on with the day. But I also know that for someone facing a serious physical disability or illness, giving in to that mindset regularly is a recipe for depression and failure. The reality of my life is that I have no arms or legs, and I need a wheelchair to navigate the world. I need assistance to accomplish some of life's most basic tasks: eating, going to the bathroom, bathing, getting dressed. Nevertheless, I have always been determined to maximize my independence, and I am fortunate that the people who raised me, and who were on my team from the day I was born, understood the importance of fostering a competitive spirit within me.

The first time I saw Coach Pierleoni standing in front of his quarterbacks holding up a finger and shouting at them, "Move your feet!" I was struck by how similar it was to the drills I'd been doing my entire life. I understood not just the process but the rationale behind the process. I knew *why* the drill made sense and what each player could get out of it. I knew it better than the players themselves. I knew it in my bones.

Admittedly, when supervising this particular drill, I lacked a fundamental piece of equipment. And I'm not talking about a coach's whistle—I actually had one of those! I'm talking about fingers. Unlike Coach Pierleoni, I couldn't instruct the quarterback to shout out the number of fingers I was holding up. So, on the spot, I devised a different strategy.

"If I look up at the sky, that's one," I explained. "If I look to my right, that's two. If I look down, that's three. And if I look to the left, that's four. Everyone got it?"

They all nodded.

"Okay, let's get started."

This complicated the drill a bit, as the players, with feet churning, had to think for a moment before shouting out the correct number, as I moved my head around on a swivel.

"Two . . . One . . . Four . . . Three!"

This went on for several minutes, while Coach Pierleoni was walking from station to station. Eventually, he returned to the quarterbacks. I wasn't sure how he'd respond since I hadn't asked permission to run the drill, but Coach P said nothing. He stood about ten feet away, hands at his side, whistle dangling from his neck. He never reached for the whistle. Instead, he watched for a minute or two, then went to the next station. There was no public affirmation, no "Great job, Robert!" Certainly, that would be a more heartwarming story. But this is football, and football players (and coaches) often do their best to hide their feelings. And I preferred it that way. By offering no comment whatsoever, he sent a clear message: Mendez is getting the job done, and it's not that big of a deal because I'd expect nothing less.

Rather than stopping practice and patting me on the back in front of everyone—Hey, look, the kid in the wheelchair figured out how to run a drill!—he quietly moved on. He knew the drill was in good hands. There was no need to say anything. This, to me, was the epitome of acceptance.

•   •   •

That summer I fell in love with football, and not just from the vantage point of a fan, someone who liked watching games on TV or playing PS4 with his friends. Football is the most complex and intricate of team sports, with a seemingly endless variety of offensive and defensive schemes and sets and plays. Coaches in all sports work long, hard hours, but football is notorious for requiring the greatest amount of homework and the highest level of organization on the part of a head coach. I became obsessed with strategy and play calling. Some of this stemmed from years of playing video games and creating complicated offensive sets and game plans. Video games (*Madden* in particular) had long represented virtual access to the sport, and now I was part of the real thing. Maybe I couldn't play, and I was definitely too young to be a real coach, but I had something to offer: a deep curiosity about the technical aspects of the game.

I was fortunate that Coach Pierleoni not only indulged that curiosity but offered avenues to further my growth and education about football. On weekends in the late spring and summer, some of the varsity guys would travel around the Bay Area to play in seven-on-seven flag football tournaments. San Jose, Salinas, San Matteo—every weekend, it seemed, they were at a different event. Since these tournaments were unaffiliated with the school district, the players had to provide their own transportation. In part because I had friends on the team, but also because he knew how much I loved football,

Coach P invited me to join the team whenever they went to these tournaments.

Travel isn't simple for me, and never has been. My chair is a highly sophisticated, mechanized piece of equipment. You don't just fold it up and toss it in the trunk. Fortunately, some of my friends drove pickup trucks, so we'd put my chair in the bed, and then, as often as not, I'd ride with Coach P and a couple of the quarterbacks. We'd talk strategy and theory all the way from Gilroy to Pacifica, or wherever we were headed. The cool thing wasn't just that I felt like part of the team but that my teammates—and more importantly, Coach P—respected my knowledge and input. These were highway skull sessions, and for me they were every bit as important as time spent in a classroom.

At first Coach P might have found it amusing or endearing that I was such a big football fan, but after a while, he came to understand that I was more than a fan, and when it came to offensive strategy, I knew my stuff.

This speaks to something that has been crucial to my life, but that is probably applicable to almost everyone on some level: the importance of believing in yourself—and being willing to demonstrate that belief through action. Humility is an important character trait. I hope I've already made it clear how many people have played vital roles in my life; how family members, friends, teachers, coaches, and mentors were willing to extend a hand when I needed it and expected more of me that I might have expected of myself. At the same time, I know how it feels to be prejudged, to have artificial limits imposed on me based solely on my appearance.

Hey, I understand—you look at a guy in a wheelchair, with no arms or legs, and you're struck first by pity and then relief. "Thank God that's not me!" you might say to yourself, as you think of all the things I can't do rather than what I can do. Or what I might be able to do, if presented with the opportunity. Not everyone responds this way, but it's the default response for many. Consequently, I've learned the value of self-advocacy, of speaking up and stepping up. I've never done this in an obnoxious or arrogant manner (at least I hope not). Indeed, I've become attuned to the importance of putting those around me at ease, because many times, my initial encounters are awkward, as those who meet me don't know what to say. I can see it in their eyes: a look of discomfort, if not sadness. It's as if they're trying hard to bite their tongue, to not say the first thing that pops into their head: I'm sorry.

I take it upon myself to lighten the mood, to let them know that I'm not only okay but that I'm a happy and well-adjusted guy, challenges notwithstanding. Sometimes it's a matter of the other person not knowing how to react upon introduction. Can't shake hands, hugging is too intimate, a pat on the back is condescending. Where does that leave you? It leaves you fidgeting, with hands in your pockets. I recognize this immediately and try to shift the burden.

"Give me a fist bump," I'll say, offering up a shoulder and an invisible fist. Invariably, the other person hesitates, then smiles and reciprocates.

After that, all is good. We're just two people having a conversation.

A lifetime of this has taught me the importance of not being fooled by appearances and not making quick assumptions. Any time I meet someone, I try to remember that we have more commonalities than differences. We are all part of God's vast and diverse family, united by our humanity.

That said, sometimes you must speak up to make your point. I will be forever grateful for the way Coach Pierleoni took me under his wing and nurtured my love of football, and how much he taught me about the *X*s and *O*s of the game. But as my dad has told me on more than one occasion, "Don't sell yourself short. You put yourself in that position. You did that. You made it happen."

He's right. That day at practice, if I hadn't summoned the nerve to run a drill when Coach P walked away, if I hadn't risked alienating my friends, and the humiliation that went with it, maybe I never would have gotten a chance to run a quarterback drill. Maybe I would have remained nothing more than a team manager. I don't know. I like to think that eventually I would have gotten an opportunity to show what I could do, but perhaps it would have taken far longer, and in the interim, I might have lost interest in football.

I took a chance. I put myself on the line. I took the road less traveled, as they say, and that made all the difference.

In the fall of my junior year, roughly two games into the season, I grew restless with my game-day role. I still enjoyed cheering on my teammates and friends, and it was fun to drive onto the field with the kicking tee, but I longed for a path to more active participation. I didn't want to appear selfish or unreasonable, but I was driven by a curiosity about what I considered the "game within the game": the chess match between competing coaches.

A typical spectator sees only the action on the field. But much is happening outside the lines—for example, constant communication between the head coach, offensive coordinator, and quarterback coach, as they develop and modify game plans in the heat of battle.

When I started hanging out on the sidelines during games, I'd gravitate toward my friends. I wanted to feel like a player. But I wasn't a player, and I never would be. I then began to pay attention to the incessant chatter of the coaches, who seemed to speak a language all their own. I'd surreptitiously move my wheelchair to a place within earshot and eavesdrop throughout the game.

I wanted to know: Are they seeing what I'm seeing? Do they view the game differently?

I began to imagine what plays I'd call if I were the offensive coordinator.

Play-action pass on third-and-one? Sure! Why not?

During these inner monologues, I tended to be overly aggressive and pass happy, which didn't always correspond with what happened on the field. In time I gained a better appreciation for tactical patience (although I still love an aerial attack). I saw the value of a varied and unpredictable game plan.

One day during practice, I got up the nerve to approach Coach Pierleoni with a request that could have been construed as unreasonable.

"Hey, Coach. Do you think maybe I could wear a headset during the game, just so I can listen to what you're saying, and the plays you're calling?"

Coach P didn't even hesitate.

"Sure, Robert. Why not?"

●   ●   ●

I did this for a few games, and I loved it! It was like being exposed to a whole different world, a secret world with its own language and rules of engagement. Knowing what call had been made, and why, gave me an entirely different perspective to the game. I felt like an insider.

But I wanted more.

"Hey, Coach," I said one day before practice.

"Yes, Robert," Coach P responded, patient as ever.

"I have a request."

"Uh-huh."

"Don't say no right away. Just think about it. Please."

"Spit it out, Robert."

"I was wondering if . . . maybe . . . I could call a few plays play during a game."

Coach P didn't speak. If this wasn't an unreasonable request, it was on the edge of being unreasonable. And I knew it. I wanted to try anyway. I decided to plead my case further by putting it in a context that might seem less unreasonable.

"Just a couple of plays," I said. "One or two. Okay . . . maybe three or four. But I'm talking about late in the game, and only if we're way ahead."

Again, no response.

"So far ahead that I can't possibly screw it up."

Coach Pierleoni sighed. "You're going to have ask the boss about this one, Robert."

The boss was Darren Yafai, Gilroy's head varsity coach. He was also a nice guy who liked having me around, but I wasn't as close to him as I was to Coach

P. Still, I understood. Handing over play-calling duties to a high school junior—if only briefly and when the game is completely in hand—is highly unusual. Also, I didn't want them to say yes just because they felt sorry for me. I wanted them to give me a chance because they knew I was passionate about football and had been studying the playbook, and that I might have a different perspective. In some small way, it would have been a furthering of my internship.

We walked over to Coach Yafai, and I repeated my sales pitch.

"Gotta be at least a two-touchdown lead," I said. "And no more than two minutes left on the clock. If it's closer than that, I won't even ask."

We had a very good team my junior year, which beat a lot of teams in our conference before losing in the semifinals of the district playoffs. I knew there was a good chance my proposed scenario would come to pass, probably more than once. Coach Pierleoni and Coach Yafai talked it over.

"I'll let you know," Coach Yafai said.

"Does that mean yes?"

"It means I'll let you know."

I didn't have to wait long, maybe a couple of games, before an opportunity presented itself. It was late in the fourth quarter when Coach Pierleoni called me over. He was standing alongside our quarterback, Chris, as the offense prepared to take the field.

"You're up, Robert."

I gave the instructions to Chris. He nodded and jogged away, then took his usual place at the front of the offensive huddle. I saw him repeat my instructions—a simple running play—and then everyone clapped a single time as they broke the huddle. After the play, I looked at Coach P.

"All yours," he said.

I called the next play, and the one after that. Then we punted, and shortly thereafter the game ended. We lined up and shook hands with the other team, and everyone headed to the locker room. A few guys congratulated me, but no one made a big deal about it.

I preferred it that way. I had done my job. Just like a real coach. Nothing special about it. All I'd needed was a chance.

CHAPTER SIX

O n November 24, 2004, a story appeared in the *Gilroy Dispatch* under the headline "A Life of Joy." This was the day before Thanksgiving, and the story effectively provoked a sense of gratitude and optimism. It was, ostensibly, my life story, or at least a small slice of it. Roughly a thousand words about a high school kid overcoming adversity through determination, love, and friendship. It was relentlessly upbeat and accompanied by thoughtful comments from friends, family members, teachers, and coaches. The lead photo depicted my buddy Nick bending over and giving me a hug, the two of us wearing our Gilroy football jerseys.

It was a nice story. Perfectly sweet and mostly accurate, focusing as it did on my belief (then as now) that

I wasn't special or unique, that I was just a normal kid—albeit one who happened to have been born without limbs. Which, admittedly, is rather unusual.

But the thing about being a teenager is that normalcy includes periods of turbulence and trauma. I love kids. I love being around young men on the cusp of adulthood and watching them fight and struggle to find their place in the world, as they try to harness all that raging adolescent energy and passion. As I write this, I am thirty-two years old, and I remember vividly what it was like to be a teenager, to feel every emotion with a white-hot intensity. Whether you're able-bodied or in a wheelchair, growing up is a glorious and frequently painful struggle. Everyone makes mistakes, including me. That's part of the journey.

I wasn't a bad kid, but I also wasn't the paragon of virtue and positivity depicted in that holiday story. The sad parts were left out; the parts about needing help with basic bodily functions and daily tasks were glossed over. I read the story and felt almost guilty:

I want to get to know this kid—he's a saint!

I was far from saintly. I was a typical teenager who hung out with the jocks and would have been a jock himself if not for some rather obvious and insurmountable obstacles. But make no mistake: that was my world, the world of sports and locker rooms and hanging out with the guys and partying on weekends, and playing video games, and doing just well enough in school to stay out of trouble. This, incidentally, isn't the path I recommend to my players, whom I urge to strive for greatness, and to push and challenge themselves, both in the classroom and on the playing field. Even so, I recognize adolescence as an adventure that is simultaneously exhilarating and confusing; few kids sail through the process unscathed. A great number of ills, however, can be mitigated by remembering one guiding principle:

Try to be a thoughtful, compassionate person.

That's it. If you can do that, then when you screw up—and you *will* screw up—people are more likely to be there to catch you or to help you get back on your feet, because they know you're worth it.

It's true that I had a lot of friends in high school. It's true that I was involved in multiple extracurricular activities and that I was generally an enthusiastic, upbeat kid liked by his peers and (most) teachers. It's also true that I coasted through a lot of my classes, content to get Cs and Bs when I was capable of getting As. It's true that I was a bit of a class clown, the kind of kid who could disrupt a class if he got on a roll with his comedy routine. Looking back on it, I know I sometimes took advantage of my position as both a local semicelebrity and a student with a significant disability. This is something most people with physical challenges don't like to talk about, because it doesn't fit the underdog narrative. But if I were so inclined, I knew I could use my disability to my advantage in certain situations.

Simply put: no one wants to yell at the kid in the wheelchair.

People tended to feel sorry for me, and because of that, I could get away with behavior that would cause other students to be dealt with immediately and harshly. I'm not talking about being hostile or overtly disrespectful but about general foolishness—taking the stage away from the teacher, for example. Some teachers let me get away with this sort of nonsense more often than they should have. Others didn't. There was one young social studies teacher whom I tested repeatedly. He was in his early twenties and inexperienced. He put up with it for a while and then began regularly kicking me out of class. This was not one of my finer moments, and I'm embarrassed to talk about it. But at the time? I just wanted to get a laugh from my classmates.

One time I was traveling to a beach bonfire and party with a bunch of my friends. There were six of us in a car that had a legal maximum of five passengers. We didn't even bring my wheelchair. I was going to hang out on the beach like everyone else. Along the way, the police pulled us over. The cop was going to ticket the driver for exceeding the passenger limit, but I quickly intervened.

"Officer, I'm sorry—this is all my fault. My mom is trying to find a new car seat for me, but we don't have one right now; so when I go out, I have to be held between two people like this."

The officer shined his light around the car, not saying much of anything. He kept the light on me for a minute, and I could almost feel his heart melting.

"Okay," he said. "You kids just be careful."

Off we went to the beach, the car filled with laughter, and everyone patting me on the back.

I realize this doesn't exactly make me a criminal, but I do regret behaving this way. I regret lying or being unappreciative, dishonest, or disrespectful; I was raised to be the opposite of those things. My point is to illustrate that I was no better or worse than most kids at that age. I could be endearing one minute and annoying the next. I didn't try to hurt anyone. I tried to remember that my actions reflected upon my family, for better or worse, and that I didn't live in a vacuum. Most of my missteps were small and benign.

But one did have lasting consequences.

And with the consequences came one huge and unexpected benefit. Strange the way life works sometimes.

• • •

I was sixteen and still a junior in high school when I got caught shoplifting at the Gilroy Outlets. I'd already held two retail jobs at the mall, at a Puma store and an Adidas store, so I knew my way around the place. I also had the benefit of being viewed as a reliable worker and an honest young man. All of this I used to my advantage during a brief and misguided walk on the wild side. Worse, I used the sympathy and trust provoked by the sight of the wheelchair, as well as the chair itself, which, in the wrong hands, can be both a getaway vehicle and an ideal hiding place for stolen goods.

Or so it seemed to me and a handful of my friends on the football team.

The plan was both simple and knuckleheaded: we'd stroll into the Sunglass Hut and try on an assortment of shades. While I was styling and posing with one of my buddies, and willfully distracting and charming the store clerk, our accomplices would lift a few handfuls of glasses from the wall displays and stuff them into one of my chair compartments. Then we'd all leave. Who would notice, right? And who would suspect the kid in the wheelchair of being a thief?

As we strolled away from the store, we all acted like we'd pulled off the heist of the century. I can still remember the adrenaline coursing through my body, a cheap thrill that quickly gave way to searing regret. By the time I got home, I felt like crap. The rush that came from doing something risky, thus gaining a measure of "street cred" in the eyes of my friends, was short-lived. I soon saw the stunt as a poor attempt at validation. Guilt interrupted my sleep that night, and I vowed silently to never steal anything again.

Please, God. I'm sorry. Just don't let anyone find out.

If I'd been truly contrite and mature, I would have returned the glasses and acknowledged my misdeed. But that would have meant implicating others, and there was no way I was going to do that. I may not have been cut out for a life of crime, but neither was I strong enough to risk friendships by doing the right thing. This is another truism of adolescence: peer pressure is not only a real thing, it is often the most important thing.

As it happened, at school Monday morning, the decision was taken out of my hands, when I was called to the principal's office. My father was there, along with a couple of officers from the Gilroy Police Department. Someone at the Sunglass Hut had noticed the missing merchandise shortly after we left the store. They had alerted the authorities and given them a description: a group of high school kids that included one boy in an elevated motorized wheelchair, one they recognized as being an employee of another store in the mall.

It was easy enough to connect the dots, but one more thing had piqued the police's interest: a few weeks earlier, the local newspaper had published that feature story about my involvement with the Gilroy High School football team. With the story came a degree of local notoriety, so when the police were given my description as a shoplifting suspect, they went straight to the school administration. The principal knew right away it was me, along with a group of Gilroy football players. And we all were in deep trouble.

Today, relating this story causes me shame, even all these years later. I regret not being stronger and smarter. I regret being selfish and stupid. Most of all, I regret being responsible for the look on my father's face when I entered the principal's office. A look not just of anger but of deep disappointment.

I didn't try to lie my way out of it or make any excuses. I apologized tearfully and waited for my punishment. They could have pressed charges. They could have suspended me from school. They could have kicked me off the football team. But they didn't do any of those things. Instead, we were ordered to make restitution for the merchandise we stole. And we were given community service. Under the circumstances, we got off easy. I'm not sure why. Maybe because they knew we were basically good kids who'd done a stupid thing. Or perhaps it had something to do with feeling sorry for me because I was in a wheelchair. Regardless, we were given a pass. I can't speak for the other guys, but I never did anything like that again.

Given my physical condition, the options for community service were somewhat limited. I couldn't pick up trash along the highway or anything like that.

"What can you do to be of service?" one of the cops asked me.

"Um . . . I don't know," I stammered. "I like to coach."

He nodded. "All right. We'll be in touch."

*　*　*

That year I coached a full season of Little League baseball. (I wasn't the head coach; I was an assistant paired with an adult who also happened to be·the father of one of the players.) The kids were nine and ten years old. They were adorable, energetic, and utterly unfiltered.

"That's a cool chair, Coach."

"Thanks."

How fast does it go?"

"Fast enough."

And so on.

I didn't expect to enjoy coaching Little League as much as I did. The kids' excitement was infectious. They loved playing ball. They were competitive. And I got to help them become better players and teammates. I couldn't believe how quickly each practice would go by, two hours melting away in a heartbeat.

During games, I served as the third-base or first-base coach—until my chair got hit by a foul line drive. A little higher and it would have hit me in the head. From that point on, I coached from the dugout.

The team did well that season. We won more games than we lost, and the kids had a lot of fun. It was a transformative experience for me. I liked the camaraderie, the excitement of being an integral part of a team. I liked being a coach. A teacher. This was different than helping with quarterback drills on Gilroy varsity. In that capacity I was more manager and friend than I was a coach. You can't expect a bunch of high school kids to treat a peer as a coach. It was fun and interesting and helped satisfy my curiosity about strategy as well as my desire to be a bigger part of the team. But the inescapable reality was that I wasn't a real coach. You can't party with a bunch of guys on Saturday night and be respected as a coach at Monday's practice. Doesn't happen. Can't happen. And I was comfortable with that.

Coaching these eager and wide-eyed little kids was different. I was compelled to behave in a manner more mature than I was. They looked up to me. They listened to me. If I explained something to them, they tried to understand it. They looked to me for advice and guidance. It gave me a real sense of importance and leadership. I was *Coach Rob*. I know it was only Little League baseball, but I liked the sound of that title, and I enjoyed the responsibility that came with it. I took it seriously.

As a coach today, one thing I continue to stress is the familial nature of sports. I want my teams to work as a unit and treat one another like brothers (or brothers and sisters, since many youth sports are now coed).

"Let's be a family," I'll say. "Let's love each other and care for each other."

I try to be a strong role model. I want my players to know I love them and care about them as people, not just as athletes. That's so important when you're dealing with kids. And the more you give them, the more you get in return. All of this started for me when I was still a "kid" myself. When I saw one of my Little League players exhibiting a selfish or otherwise negative attitude, I confronted him. Not in an angry or authoritarian way, but in a manner I hoped would convey a sense of care and concern.

"The way you are behaving is wrong. The way you are treating your teammates is wrong. You can do better than this."

Invariably, they did do better. They wanted to please their coaches and be better teammates. They just needed direction, and I was honored and excited to be one of the people who might help steer them in the right direction. And, of course, I enjoyed the games. I liked competing. I'd always been that way, but now I understood coaching to be about something more than wins and losses. It was about teaching and mentoring.

For the first time, I thought, "Maybe I can do this. Maybe I won't be relegated to the broadcast booth. Maybe there's a place for me on the sideline."

I do quite a bit of public speaking now, and often I'm asked to address school and church groups. I don't shy away from the shoplifting incident, in part because I want the audience to know that everyone makes mistakes. It's what you learn from those mistakes, and how you atone for them, that counts the most. I tell kids, "Try not to lose yourself. Stay grounded. Rely on faith and family and friends you trust." It's fairly simple. There are consequences to every decision, and the bad ones pile up fast. After a while, it becomes difficult to recover. I got lucky. A bad decision led to consequences but also to an unexpected opportunity: a chance to be a "real" coach. Over time, that brief introduction evolved into a lifelong passion. A seed had been planted.

Convincing others that I might have the aptitude and ambition to coach was a challenge that required perseverance and patience. I never wanted a handout or any special consideration. I asked only that I be given an equal opportunity to show what I could do. When I was a high school senior, I continued working with the quarterbacks on the Gilroy varsity team. Technically speaking, I was still just a manager (and that is without question the way my friends perceived me), but I thought of myself as more of an assistant coach. I would run the guys through drills and workouts. I would draw up plays. Despite having never played a single down of organized football, I knew how to help them get better at their positions.

I just knew.

* * *

It helped that I had a strong work ethic (even if I sometimes lacked focus in the classroom). In the summer before my senior year, I took a new job at Best Buy, where I was already somewhat well-known as a regular customer who liked to hang out in the electronics and gaming departments. One day, I went into the store with my parents because my father needed to get his printer repaired. While we waited, he struck up a conversation with one of the assistant managers, a nice guy named Ariel.

"Hey, by any chance are you guys hiring?" my father asked.

"Yeah, we're always looking for good people," Ariel responded. "You should talk to Adrian; he's the sales manager."

So we tracked down Adrian, and this time, I did the talking. I introduced myself and asked if there were any open sales positions. Adrian gave me a long, quizzical look, almost like he thought I was messing with him.

"For who?" he finally said.

I looked up at my dad, who betrayed not a hint of emotion.

"For me."

There was a long pause as Adrian's expression changed from befuddlement to embarrassment, and, finally, to professionalism. None of which I took personally. By this point I'd experienced enough interactions defined by preconceived notions related to my physical challenges that almost nothing surprised me. I wasn't easily shaken or offended. As always, the burden of proof, as well as the responsibility for making an awkward encounter more comfortable, fell on me (even though I was a high school student and Adrian was a grown man).

"Oh . . . um . . . I'm sorry."

"No worries, man. Your boss said you might be hiring. I was wondering if I could fill out an application."

"Sure. Come with me."

I'd already been working in retail for a couple of years and had good recommendations, so I got the job. I'd like to say I was hired entirely on my own merits, based on prior experience and because I demonstrated an honest and sincere desire to be part of the Best Buy team. But it's probably also true that hiring someone with such an obvious disability, then giving that person the support to succeed, would be a positive experience for everyone. It would be good for my self-esteem, for the customers who benefited from my legitimate knowledge of the product line, and for Best Buy's corporate image. I don't mean to imply that they were cynical. Not at all. I think they were progressive. I've been a coach long enough to understand the importance of empowering people and placing them in positions in which their talents can be utilized to the fullest.

As a coach, I feel good when I do that, and I know the players feel good about themselves as well. I'd assume the same symbiotic relationship applies in the corporate world. You pay it forward.

I started out in the gaming department, my dream assignment. I got to spend hours in a sea of video games, consoles, headsets, and screens. When a new game or piece of equipment was released, I was able to try it out. Predictably, sometimes customers expressed trepidation over my supposed credentials.

What can this guy know about video games? Obviously, he's never played. You need hands to play Xbox or PlayStation. Right?

Wrong.

"Give me the controller," I said on more than one occasion. "Put it under my chin."

The customer, usually a boy in his teens or early twenties, would oblige uncomfortably and then look on with stupefaction as I gave a demonstration. I wasn't trying to show off or make anyone feel bad. As I said, I had already accrued a lifetime of experience in diffusing uncomfortable situations and convincing others that things aren't always as they appear. Still, it was fun to see their reactions.

"Whoa . . . Dude."

In September, my supervisor and I concocted a plan to promote the release of the newest version of *Madden* on both PlayStation and Xbox. *Madden* was among the most popular video games and easily the biggest sports game. The annual release of a new version was an event, with much speculation about which player would be on the cover, what improvements in graphics and design there would be, and of course, how much it would cost. This was before gamers routinely downloaded digital versions of their favorite games, and before online gaming became standard. When a new game was issued, there was furious competition among customers, many of whom would preorder a copy to ensure they wouldn't be shut out and have to wait weeks to play with their friends.

We decided to capitalize on the anticipated *Madden* frenzy by hosting a tournament. The rules were straightforward: thirty-two players, head-to-head competition, single elimination. To compete in the tournament, you had to purchase a copy of *Madden* at our store and then fill out an entry form. We then held a lottery to select the thirty-two entrants (out of more than a hundred applicants) who would take part in the tournament. There were no age restrictions or requirements; the tournament field included entrants as young as eleven or twelve, and others in their forties. Although I came up with the idea, I had no role in selecting the final field or assigning brackets; however, I was granted a wild card entry as a participant. First prize was a hundred-dollar Best Buy gift card. Second place received a less valuable gift card. The remaining proceeds were donated to charity.

The tournament began on a Saturday afternoon, in the home theater section of the store, and continued for nearly eight hours, until well past closing time. I breezed through the first few rounds, winning by margins of thirty and forty points. My friends and family were accustomed to seeing how adept I was at video games, but to the casual spectators that day—and especially to my opponents—it must have been a shock. I even got the feeling that the first guy felt sorry for me and was prepared to go easy in the hope of not running up the score. Midway through the first quarter I had a two-touchdown lead, and his jaw was on the floor.

How the hell am I losing a video game to a kid with no arms?!

Even my coworkers were stunned. They hung out with me every day, and a few of them had seen me mess around with the controller, but they'd never seen me play a competitive game of *Madden*. It's safe to say I had the biggest cheering section of anyone in the tournament.

The element of surprise wasn't a factor in the championship game. On the other controller was my friend Jay, a teammate on the football team. Jay and I had played about a thousand hours of *Madden* against each other. He knew my strengths, and I knew his. There would be no quarter given by either of us. Pride was at stake. The winner would have bragging rights at football practice the next day. He'd also have a hundred-dollar gift card.

Considering that the store had closed by the time the championship game was played, there remained a decent crowd of spectators. Several employees hung out to watch, as did tourney participants who'd been eliminated in the earlier rounds. It was a good game. I was driving late in the fourth quarter and had a chance to take the lead, but Jay intercepted a pass and ran it all the way back for a game-clinching touchdown as time ran out.

"Sorry, bro," Jay said with a smile. "Good game, though."

"You too, man."

We exchanged a fist bump and accepted our prizes. I was proud of my performance and even more proud that the event had been such a big success. And if I had to lose to someone, I was glad it was one of my teammates.

It was a good day.

CHAPTER SEVEN

graduated from Gilroy High School in 2006 and began the transition to adulthood, as did the rest of my friends and classmates. I'd like to say I pursued my dream of becoming a head football coach with laser-like focus, but that wouldn't be the truth. Like a lot of young adults, my journey toward finding purpose and fulfillment was marked by missteps and hesitation. This had nothing to do with my physical challenges but rather with my uncertainty about what I wanted to do with my life, and the complicated process of growing up.

I didn't lack ambition. I just hadn't yet figured out how to channel that ambition in a way that would lead to accomplishing tangible goals. I was spread too thin.

To encourage a sense of privacy and autonomy, my bedroom at my parents' house was separated from

WHO SAYS I CAN'T?

the main house by a long hallway, and it had its own bathroom and a private entrance from the backyard. Friends often stopped by and hung out until well into the night, or they'd pick me up and we'd go out. Normal stuff for an eighteen-year-old. But I was far from a slacker. I also enrolled in a full load of classes at Gavilan College and continued to work at least twenty to twenty-five hours a week at Best Buy. Sandwiched between all of this, in the fall, I served as an assistant coach of the Gilroy freshman football team; my title was "quarterbacks' coach."

This would be a crowded schedule for even an able-bodied young man. For me, it was almost too much. I had an aide and my family's help, but I didn't want to rely on others for everything. So most days, I traveled on my own, from home to school to job. How did I do this? In my wheelchair, for the most part. I'd load up my chair with whatever supplies I needed and then head out the door for a roughly three-mile ride to school. The first part of the trip wasn't bad, on suburban streets with wide shoulders—it wasn't much different or more dangerous than riding a bike. But the last mile or so was quite congested, with lots of busy intersections and traffic whistling by at forty to fifty miles per hour.

It wasn't unusual for drivers to honk their horns or wave as they went by. Thanks to the story in the *Gilroy Dispatch*, I remained a minor celebrity in my hometown. Of course, there also weren't many young men driving motorized wheelchairs around Gilroy. If you saw one, it was likely to be me.

Depending on when classes ended, I'd ride to either Best Buy or Gilroy High School for football practice. The trip to Best Buy was particularly perilous because it included crossing a highway on-ramp with no bike lane or stop signal. I'd have to wait until there was a big gap in traffic—I got pretty good at estimating the speed of oncoming cars—and then hit the gas, so to speak. This wasn't the only way to get to Best Buy, but it was the most expedient, and since a typical charge on my wheelchair battery was good for only about eight to ten miles a day, I always took the shortest possible routes. The only other option would have been to rely entirely on rides from my parents or an aide, and for reasons of both economics and a desire for independence, I chose not to do that.

To whatever extent possible, I wanted to be in charge of my own life. That might sound somewhat reckless or selfish—indeed, when my parents heard about me playing human *Frogger* on a freeway on-ramp, they were mortified—but when you've grown up dependent on others for assistance with many of life's most basic functions, you learn to seize every opportunity for self-reliance.

Some things aren't negotiable: I can't dress myself, and I need help showering and going to the bathroom.

But I can drive the hell out of a wheelchair. It is nothing less than an extension of my own body. At that point in my life, when I was young and tireless and aggressive, I thought nothing of taking the shorter, more dangerous route to work. In part because it was the most efficient way to get the job done. And, maybe, because it made me feel a bit more alive.

Moreover, being late has consequences, which I'd known for some time. Everything takes me a little longer (or a lot longer) than it does most people, so I'm keenly aware of deadlines and the probability of meeting unforeseen obstacles while getting through the day. One afternoon, I was a few minutes late clocking in at Best Buy. I received a reprimand. Typical protocol. It didn't happen again for a few months. Then, one day, I got caught in traffic and clocked in five minutes late for my shift. I received another reprimand. The next day I got stuck again while scrambling from school to work, and clocked in seven minutes late. I knew I was in trouble; I just didn't know how severe the consequences might be. The following day, I was called into my supervisor's office and told I was being dismissed. I apologized but didn't argue. I thought the punishment was harsh, but I also knew I'd been late on consecutive days and that the store was within its right to terminate my employment. I was reluctant to use my disability—which I'd fought so hard to overcome, and which I never wanted to define me—as an excuse.

I went home and told my dad that I'd lost my job. I was embarrassed. He sort of shrugged and said, "Find another one, Robert."

And I did. In relatively short order I landed a position as a host at a Chili's restaurant, located right next door to Best Buy. It was an easy job for anyone with an outgoing personality. All you had to do was smile and make small talk with customers while directing them to their tables. I missed my job at Best Buy, but at least I was gainfully employed, and for that I was grateful.

A few months into my tenure, I seated a customer who remembered me from my previous job.

"Hi, Robert," she said. "What are you doing here?"

"Oh, things didn't work out at Best Buy," I said sheepishly. I was hoping to either change the subject or move on to the next customer, but she pressed me.

"That's too bad. I thought you liked it there."

"I did, but . . . um . . . well, I got fired."

She seemed surprised and sympathetic, and asked if I was free anytime soon to chat in greater detail. "I'd like to hear more."

We met at a coffee shop a couple days later, and I told her the whole story. I made it clear that I wasn't asking for sympathy and that I had been late for work on consecutive days.

"They probably would have done the same thing to an able-bodied person," I said.

"Maybe. And that would have been wrong too. I'd like you to talk to someone."

She put me in touch with a labor attorney who specialized in wrongful termination lawsuits. We met at a Denny's a few weeks later, and the attorney felt I had a case. I was skeptical. Not because I didn't believe her—she seemed smart and confident—but because I was reluctant to weaponize my disability. I'd spent my whole life refusing to ask for preferential treatment. On more than occasion I'd gotten angry with people who perceived me as "special" or in need of delicate handling.

Now I was going to file a lawsuit against my former employer?

"I don't know if I can do this. I mean, I was late. More than once."

"You received two warnings, months apart, and then you were terminated," she said. "That's insufficient. And it's wrong." She paused. "For *anyone.*"

The point wasn't lost on me. She wanted to represent me not as a young man with a disability whose dismissal would be bad from a public relations standpoint but as someone who had been wrongfully terminated. I missed my old job and my coworkers, and I didn't entirely disagree with her. So I consented to legal representation.

"What would you like to get out of this?" she asked.

"I just want my job back."

"That's it?"

"A raise would be nice."

She smiled. "Nothing else?"

I knew what she meant. But the thought of suing Best Buy made me queasy. I wasn't asking for a hand-out or retribution.

"Nah, that's it."

"Okay."

Within a few weeks I had left Chili's and returned to Best Buy. It was, not surprisingly, awkward at first, but that soon passed. Eventually, I increased from part-time to full-time hours, while taking classes and announcing volleyball and football games at Gavilan and coaching at Gilroy. It was an insanely ambitious schedule, made even less manageable when combined with my reluctance to forfeit an active social life.

Something had to give.

That something turned out to be school. There weren't enough hours in the day to accommodate the demands of my schedule. I didn't miss a lot of classes, but I did miss a few, and by the time I got home from work or football practice, all I wanted to do was sleep. The little spare time I did have was filled by my friends. You have to prioritize things in life, figure out what's really important to you, and at that moment in time, education was low on my priority list. I don't say that with pride, and I wouldn't advise any young person to follow my example in that regard. I'm being as honest as I possibly can. I liked my job, and I liked having a steady paycheck. It was more important to me at that time to have money in my pocket, which I associated with independence and maturity. I wasn't looking ten years down the road, trying to plan a career and assessing what education I needed. I was just trying to grow up, like the rest of my friends.

I do think it's important to note that I was never lazy. I grew up watching my father and grandfather work hard as they tried to provide for their families. Mine wasn't a family that spoke often about the value of a college degree. It wasn't denigrated in any way, but neither was it held up as the key to a bigger and better life. In my family, you rolled up your sleeves and went to work, every single day. If times got tough, you worked harder and longer. And there's real value in seeing that held up as an example of how to live your life. I'd like to see all of my players do well in school and put themselves in a position to get a college degree. In our society, I do believe that education helps break down barriers and provide opportunity. But I also know from personal experience that the journey from boy to man can be circuitous. Some people mature early, others later. Some people are lucky enough to find their life's work early, while others search for years before feeling a spark of motivation.

With that in mind, I urge my players to embrace the concept of work. Whatever you do, give it your best effort. No half measures. Do your best in the classroom and on the football field. Be an honorable, hardworking person. The rest will take care of itself.

"Eventually, you'll figure out what you want to do with your life," I tell them. "And when you do, you'll have the drive and ambition to make it happen."

* * *

I took several years off from school before resuming my studies at San Jose City College. In the meantime, I worked long hours at Best Buy and fell deeply in love with the game of football. It's interesting the way my relationship with the sport, and my commitment to coaching, evolved over time. While I enjoyed coaching Little League baseball and helping out with the program at Gilroy, there was no bolt of lightning, no single moment or episode that put me on a purpose-driven path. It was more of a slow burn, like falling in love with someone who is already a close friend. I'd coach in the fall, give it my best effort, then put the game aside for six months.

After a couple of years, an interesting thing began to happen. I'd find myself missing the game. And not missing it the way a fan might miss it. I'd be at Best Buy, pushing through another shift, and I'd find myself daydreaming about football. I don't mean in the fantastic way of a kid who pretends he's playing in the NFL. I'm talking about something more concrete: diagramming plays in my head, creating new and interesting practice drills. Sometimes a player, or a former player, would walk into the store, and we'd talk about the game and school and life. And I'd realize how much I missed it, and how I couldn't wait for the next season to come. I had long enjoyed sports in general and football in particular, but now I was becoming obsessed.

I thought, maybe this is what I should be doing with my life. Maybe I should be a coach. And not a position coach or even an offensive coordinator—a head coach. I wanted to be in charge of a team, with all the pressure and responsibility that comes with that title, and with the opportunity to impact the lives of a group of young people.

Here's the thing about coaching football: even at the high school level, it's a difficult job. The coach oversees a large staff, like a corporate CEO. He has to be a master of multitasking, but he also has to know when to delegate and whom to trust with various responsibilities. He has to be a tactician and a therapist, capable of interpreting data and motivating his team. It's a complex, exhausting, nonstop job. And if you're a high school coach, it's also only a part-time job, with long hours and little compensation. The majority of high school coaches are also teachers, so by the time they step on the football field in the afternoon, they've already put in a full day of work. They are drained. Most of the time, you'd never know it by looking at them, for coaching football is like a shot of adrenaline. You cross the white line and instantly find a second wind.

No one coaches high school football for the money. You coach because you love the game. You love the practices, the strategy, the competition, and the kids.

Especially the kids.

As I moved into my twenties and put some distance between me and the players I was coaching, I liked them even more. I thought I had something to offer. So I decided I wanted to be a head football coach.

"You know, Robert, there's not a lot of money in coaching," my father said to me one day, after I told him of my goal. (That's what it was—a goal, not just a dream.)

"I know, Dad. But money isn't everything."

A bit idealistic, perhaps. Money is important, especially if your life reasonably forecasts the possibility of catastrophic health-care expenses. But I believed then, and I believe now, that if you can find purpose and joy in your work, everything else will work out.

What I didn't realize then was how challenging it would be to secure a head coaching job, or how long it would take. You see, coaches love coaching. And there are a lot of us out there, looking for work, fighting for the best jobs. Many coaches spend years climbing the ladder before they get to run their own team at the varsity or even the junior varsity level. Complicating matters for me was that I didn't exactly fit the profile of a typical football coach. I had never played the game. I had never played any competitive sport on the high school level.

I was in a wheelchair.

I had no limbs.

I was, to put it mildly, *different.*

I would have to prove not only that I was capable of being a head coach, but that I was more capable than most. I would have to build a résumé that would negate any concern about my physical condition. In some ways this was a double-edged sword, as it often has been in my life. It's wrong for a person to be discriminated against in the hiring process (or in life, for that matter) due to a disability that in no way precludes him or her from successfully meeting the job's demands. This sometimes gets complicated. I can't be a firefighter because there's a physical component to the job that's required of every candidate. But a disability cannot legally be used as a reason for termination or as a barrier to hiring, if the candidate is otherwise suited to the job.

In other words, you can't discriminate based on appearances and preconceived notions.

Yet it happens. It happens in the workplace, and it happens in life. I know that people sometimes look at me and presume there are things I can't do. Indeed, some things I can't do; we all have barriers that can't be scaled. The difference, for me, is that my appearance too often provokes false limitations.

He wants to be a football coach? How is that even possible? He can't do that.

Who says I can't?!

 •   •   •

Like any other young coach, I paid my dues. First, I spent two years as a position coach and then offensive coordinator of the freshman team at Gilroy High. When most of the coaching staff there left to start a program at newly formed Christopher High School in Gilroy, I took a job at the Pop Warner level. I guess you could call that a demotion, but I was thankful to still be involved in the game.

In 2009, I was offered what at first felt like a dream job: junior varsity head coach at Christopher, where I'd be reunited with my former coaches. But Christopher was going through growing pains—it didn't even have a senior class yet—and numbers for football were dangerously low: twenty-two players on the JV and only eighteen on the varsity. After a few weeks of practice, the two teams were merged into one team that could play safely at the varsity level. I remained on the staff as an assistant.

I stayed at Christopher for three years, moving on to assistant positions at the JV and varsity levels at several different schools in the San Jose area. Unfortunately, transiency comes with the territory. Coaches are nomadic folks, especially early in their careers. Promotions frequently involve relocation. Sometimes you move because the head coach has resigned or been fired, and the new guy wants to bring in his own staff. I experienced all of these scenarios early in my career. You learn to be thick-skinned and professional.

But coaching is also a business of personalities, and as with any organization, sometimes people don't see eye to eye. I've never been shy about speaking my mind and standing up for what I believe is right. By the time I was named offensive coordinator for the junior varsity team at Sobrato High School in 2014, I had compiled a solid coaching résumé, bolstered by hundreds of hours at clinics and summer camps. I was confident in my ability to run an offense and eager to see what I could do in the job. We had a good season, and I enjoyed working with the kids. It was my hope to stay at Sobrato for several years, especially if there was a chance to become a head coach.

After only one season the head coach resigned, and I figured I'd have to go back on the job market again. Indeed, the new coach cleaned house, brought in a whole new staff, and initially indicated that I would be part of the purge. I didn't take it personally; it was business. But the school administration had gotten positive feedback about my performance from many JV players and their families, so the new coach was encouraged to retain my services. I became one of the few holdovers from the previous regime.

In the beginning we got along well . . . or so it seemed. We had a nice, long talk about coaching philosophy, with a particular emphasis on offensive strategy. I told him about some of the clinics I'd attended and what I'd learned. I'd gotten to know some of the coaches at Southern Methodist University (SMU), and I'd become enamored of their offensive system. As a result, by the summer of 2015, I'd begun to develop a playbook that was similar to SMU's, leaning heavily on a spread offense (quarterback in shotgun formation), frequently in "hurry-up" mode. It's an aggressive, fast-paced offense designed to keep the defense on its heels. It's also an ambitious offense for a high school team. But the head coach apparently liked it, and we agreed to develop it not just at the JV level but at the varsity level as well. As I said before, most programs like to use one playbook at all levels, so by the time the players get to the varsity team, everyone has the plays memorized. Consistency is the key.

So we were on the same page in terms of offensive strategy. But we didn't agree on much else. Some of the problem was a personality clash. Some of it, I believe, was because the varsity coach had been pressured to retain me as a coach when he would have preferred to hire his own JV offensive coordinator. In fairness to him, that's a normal response. But I also think some of it was jealousy resulting from the fact that I was a holdover from the previous regime, and a popular coach at that. Many of the new coach's varsity players had been on my JV team the previous year, and I had a strong relationship with most of them. Their parents liked me too. For whatever reason, I got the sense this didn't sit well with my boss. Maybe he felt threatened. Maybe he just didn't like me. All I know is that I did a good job that season. We won more games than we lost, and I developed a playbook that was successfully implemented across the entire program.

But one day in the off-season, I received a text from the varsity coach, informing me that my services would no longer be required.

I had been fired.

Like I said, it's business. I'd been fortunate to have had even one season with a new staff. But part of me was furious. There was no reason for me to lose my job, and none was offered. The worst part was the way the news was delivered—*by text!*

Life is about relationships, and sometimes relationships are messy. There is a right way and a wrong way to end a relationship, and texting is definitely a wrong way. I'd given two solid years to Sobrato; I had developed a playbook and earned the players' respect. I felt I was owed an explanation. In a face-to-face meeting. Or at least on a phone call.

In a fit of rage, I responded with a text of my own. I called him a coward for not giving me the courtesy of a meeting. It wasn't a nice note, and we've not spoken since. I'm not proud of letting my emotions get the best of me in that moment, but I will say this: while losing the job at Sobrato hurt, it also added fuel to the fire. I stared at that text exchange for several minutes, seething. Then, a calm came over me. I dropped the stylus from my lips and smiled.

Just watch. I'm going to prove you wrong.

CHAPTER EIGHT

One of the toughest—and most rewarding—jobs I had was at San Jose High School, where, for much of the 2016 season, I served as offensive coordinator for the junior varsity team and quarterbacks' coach for the varsity team. That fall, the San Jose *Mercury News* published a story about my experience. This level of notoriety was far beyond what I'd experienced in Gilroy, and it felt both emboldening and discomforting. It was a nice story, like the one that had appeared in my local paper a decade earlier, but I bristled somewhat at the realization that it had been published not because I was a successful football coach (which remained my goal) but because I was a limbless man who also happened to be a football coach.

It has taken me some time to come to terms with the perfectly human response people seem to have when they hear of my story—and especially when they witness visuals that accompany the story. I am a (profoundly) physically challenged man trying to make his way in a world defined by physicality. I'm not talking about the world at large (although that's true as well) but about the world of football. At the highest levels, football players are incredible athletes—spectacular physical specimens who have spent a lifetime honing their skills and sculpting their physiques. And while it's true that few coaches ever played professional football, just about everyone who coaches did play, somewhere.

I did not. I could not. That I am now a coach provokes curiosity at the least, skepticism at the worst, and wonder in the vast middle. Within the coaching fraternity there exists a long-held belief that you can't know a sport well if you've never played the game. Certainly, you can't know it well enough to teach others how to play. I'm not so arrogant as to think there's no merit to this argument. Playing football from a young age fosters a love for the sport, and an understanding of its intricacies, that not only provides a springboard to coaching but also generates a large pool of qualified candidates. But, as always, there are exceptions to the rule, and people do become outstanding coaches in a sport they've never played, or at least didn't play professionally.

In my case, skepticism rises to the level of incredulity based primarily, if not entirely, on my physical condition.

How can he explain or demonstrate a drill?

How can he navigate the practice field or the sideline in a wheelchair?

How can he diagram a play?

How?

If you've gotten this far in the narrative, then you know the answers to these questions. Nevertheless, they've been a persistent refrain in my life and career, which I understand and indulge with as much grace as I can muster. But I'm a human being, no more or less fallible than the next person, and on occasion I've lacked the maturity or patience to deal with these questions, regardless of their origin. I still don't like being defined by tetra-amelia syndrome. Yet I understand how unique it is, and I've tried to embrace the possibility that by being a successful coach and a decent human being—by showing that even profound hardship can be overcome—maybe I have something to offer the world.

Something beyond coaching (although coaching is its own reward).

On the morning of November 18, 2016 (that's right—Thanksgiving Week all over again), the *Mercury News* published a story under the following delightfully upbeat headline:

"No Arms, No Legs, No Problem: San Jose Coach Defies the Odds."

Accompanying the story was a photo of me heading off the field in my wheelchair, Starbucks cup and smartphone clearly visible, players in the background.

The story began as follows:

"Rob Mendez sounds like any other football coach on any other field across America—passionate, authoritative, knowledgeable . . ."

Cool. Good start.

". . . but he is like no other coach you know."

Here we go again.

"He has no arms or legs. He moves in a custom-made wheelchair that he operates with his shoulders. He diagrams plays on a smartphone attached to the chair, using a stylus that he maneuvers with his mouth."

Yup, been doing it for years. Is this going to be a pity party?

"He does all this with a spirit that seems to lift everyone around him—players, coaches, strangers, peers and family."

Okay, that's very sweet. Thank you.

It was a thoughtful and balanced story that touched equally on my personal and professional journey, with flattering comments from coaches all across the Bay Area with whom I'd been fortunate to work, as well as from some of my players at the time.

"He taught me better footwork," said one player.

"I'm amazed," said another.

"I didn't bring him in here to be a feel-good story," explained my boss, head coach David Ashkinaz.

For someone who wanted more than anything to be respected as a legitimate football coach, not as a charity case, this was a critical observation, and it made my heart swell with pride to see it in print.

Yet it was a feel-good story, and I had to get comfortable with that notion, because there it was, in black and white, in the words of my father:

"Robert is kind of like the light in a dark room. He's the same for us as he is for other people."

That one almost made me cry. It also felt like a heck of a burden to carry. I mean, you try being the light in a dark room for everyone who meets you. We all have bad days or bad months—or even bad years. I've had some tough days—days when my scoliosis acts up and I can't fall asleep, or when chronic bed sores on my buttocks make every movement painful, or when I have a sudden need to use the bathroom and have to ask for assistance. Even more mundane matters can spark a darkening of mood, like when we lose a football game and I question some of the decisions I made in the heat of competition.

But I'm fortunate—the cloud usually passes quickly. Like I said, when it comes to having a generally positive outlook on life, I'm one of the lucky ones. I was practically born with a smile on my face. And if that provides inspiration or perspective to someone else, then fine. I'm eager to help. I want to be of service. It just took me a little while to get to this point.

By the time the story appeared in the *Mercury News*, I had grown accustomed to the occasional request for a speaking engagement. Typically, these came from school or church groups, and the audience comprised mostly of young people. I didn't think of myself as a "motivational speaker," nor as a particularly inspirational person, but I was happy to oblige and tell my story. It never occurred to me that there might be an audience beyond the Bay Area or beyond the world of football.

On the morning of November 18, a young woman named Kristen Lappas found herself in a Bay Area coffee shop, where she saw a copy of the *Mercury News*. Kristen was a producer for ESPN, specializing in features and documentaries, so she was always on the lookout for interesting projects. Within a few weeks— after the story had been picked up by a few Bay Area news stations and began trending throughout the state—Kristen had reached out to me about the possibility of producing a short documentary about my life.

From our first conversation, I liked Kristen a lot. It was clear that she was a dedicated and passionate professional. I did some homework. Kristen and I were almost the same age. Obviously, since she worked at ESPN, she was an extremely knowledgeable sports fan. Considering that her father is Steve Lappas, a former basketball coach at Villanova and now a prominent broadcaster, it must be in her blood. But Kristen had already established her own bona fides by piling up a stack of awards.

"I want to tell your story," she said.

Kristen was ambitious, earnest, smart. I was inclined to trust her. But I told her I wanted the story to be about football as much as about my personal story.

"It's both," she explained. For that reason, she wanted to wait until I became a head coach—even at the JV level—before committing to the project. Her reasoning was sound. If we did the story while I was an assistant, and then I became a head coach in mid-production, or worse, in postproduction, they would have to start all over. I appreciated the transparency.

"I'm hoping that happens soon," I said.

"Me too."

I put that conversation out of my head almost as soon as it happened. My focus was on trying to land a head coaching position. That would prove to be a challenge. When Coach Ashkinaz resigned, there was a shake-up in the San Jose program. I'd been around long enough to know exactly what that meant: a new varsity coach would be hired, and that person would replace most of the current staff. That's the way it worked. Rather than sit around and wait for the inevitable to happen, I decided to take a big swing.

I applied for the varsity job.

I went into the process with my eyes wide open. For several reasons, I was a long-shot candidate, and none of those reasons had anything to do with being physically challenged. First, I had never been a head coach at any level, which is typically a prerequisite for taking over a varsity program. Exceptions are sometimes made if the candidate has spent a few years as a top assistant at the varsity level (as, say, an offensive or defensive coordinator). I couldn't check that box. Second, I was part of the prior regime, and that regime had won only nine games in three years. It was perfectly reasonable for the administration to seek someone who would provide a completely new perspective. A fresh start, so to speak.

Nevertheless, I submitted a formal application. I was granted an interview. It was courteous and professional. I did not get the job.

So, as 2016 gave way to 2017, a little more than a month after that uplifting story appeared in the *Mercury News*, I was out of work.

Again.

There was no point in sulking. You control what you can control in life, and this situation, like so many others in coaching, was well beyond my sphere of influence. I cleaned up my résumé, got on the phone, and started looking for a new job. The search proved more challenging than I'd anticipated, but I wound up with what appeared to be a pretty good offer: offensive coordinator at Overfelt High School in San Jose. This was a chance to develop a playbook and direct an offense at the varsity level, a necessary step on the road to becoming a head coach. I was excited and grateful. But it turned out to be a painful learning experience with an unpleasant end.

For three months, in late spring and summer of 2017, we implemented a spread offense. We did this for two reasons: one, it's a fun and proven high-scoring offense at every level. I like teaching it, and kids like to play it. Second, our roster featured an athletic, mobile quarterback with a good arm, the most vital component of a spread offense. To be effective, you need a quarterback who can get out of the pocket and run, see the field, and be ready to throw from any angle. We had that. Moreover, a spread offense is predicated on speed and intelligence and versatility, and therefore, it can help mitigate shortcomings in size and muscle. Ultimately, we had plenty of size, but you never know what might happen as a season progresses. In my mind, the spread offense gave us the best chance to win games.

To my dismay, the head coach disagreed. In the first week of the regular season, he decided that the spread offense wouldn't work. He wanted to switch to a more traditional power offense with tight formations. Run, run, run. Off-tackle left, off-tackle right. Hammer the middle of the line and pass only when necessary.

I was dumbfounded. While a power offense can be effective with the right personnel and training, in my view it was ill suited for our lineup. We had a couple of big running backs, but our quarterback was exceptional, and we were deliberately going to neutralize him. More importantly, we had spent three months implementing a spread offense. Now, right when the season began, we were going to throw out all the preparation and start over? We were going to bet the whole season on an offense our kids hadn't even learned or practiced?

It was arrogant. It was irresponsible. That's how I saw it, anyway.

And that's the opinion I expressed.

One could argue that an offensive coordinator's job is to do what the head coach tells him to do. But in this case, I believed strongly that the coach was wrong, that his plan was both unfair and doomed to fail. I'd been hired to run the offense, and our kids had spent three months learning that offense. They loved it, and they understood it.

"Coach, this is a bad idea," I said one day before practice, in the coaches' offices. "We'll get killed."

He disagreed. I held my ground. A discussion escalated into an argument, loud enough for the other coaches to hear.

"It's your team," I eventually said. "Do what you want. But I won't be part of it."

I left the office, rolled right out to the players, took a deep breath, and explained what had happened, while trying to maintain my composure.

"I love you guys," I said. "And I'm sorry. But I can't work with Coach anymore."

Over the next few days, I received email messages, phone calls, and texts from many of the players, as well as from their parents, asking me to reconsider. But there was no undoing what had been done. I felt bad about leaving the players, but I believed I'd made the right professional and ethical decision. Coaching, to me, is all about the kids. In this case, I felt like I was working for a self-centered coach who put himself ahead of the players. I couldn't do it.

There were consequences to taking a stand, however: I was out of work again. Fortunately, I quickly found a job coaching with a friend at the Pop Warner level (the same program in which I'd coached a few years earlier). It was a step back, but at least it was fun, and it allowed me to continue to work with kids and stay in the game. I never lost faith.

*   *   *

One day in the spring of 2018, I was hanging out in a local Starbucks, perusing a website that serves as a clearinghouse for almost every public education job in the Bay Area, including coaching positions. At the time, I was working at a call center, offering tech support and instruction to customers who'd purchased various products and then went home and discovered they had no idea how to assemble or operate said product. It was a good job that offered the flexibility of working in an office or from home. Or from a coffee shop, which is where I was now, on my lunch break, trying to figure out how I would get back into high school coaching.

Since the logistics of commuting are more challenging for me than they are for most people, I tried to limit my search to a radius of thirty miles from my home in Gilroy. One of the openings was for a job as head coach of the junior varsity program at Prospect High School in Saratoga. This didn't fit the geographic requirement (it was nearly forty miles away), but it seemed like too good of an opportunity to pass up. Prospect was a big school that had superb facilities and played in a competitive league. By any reasonable measure, it was an exceptional job. Most important of all, it was a chance to be a head coach.

I'd been around the game long enough to know that there would be stiff competition. So I immediately filled out the online application, attached a résumé, and modified a template letter I had on standby for whenever I found an attractive job. As you might expect of any big organization, the application didn't go to the athletic director or even to the varsity head football coach (who oversees the whole program) but rather to the human resources department of the Campbell Union School District. I knew that if I just hit "send" on the online application and crossed my fingers, there would be little chance of my résumé climbing out of an electronic stack of a hundred similarly qualified applicants. I made a few calls and got the email address of the varsity head coach, Mike Cable. Then I wrote him a long note, introducing myself and explaining why I wanted the job, and why I thought I would be a solid addition to his staff.

Then I waited. A week went by. Two weeks. No response.

I decided to call the school because I knew that Coach Cable was also a physical education teacher. Maybe I could get him to pick up the phone.

No luck. Straight to voice mail.

After a couple days went by, I figured I was out of the running. Coaching is one of the ultimate networking gigs, and more often than not hires are made based on an established relationship or a recommendation from someone who knows the applicant. Talent and experience are required, but they aren't always enough to get you through the door. I had never met anyone on the staff at Prospect, so the odds weren't in my favor.

I had already turned my attention to other job openings when my phone rang one morning.

"Hi, I'm trying to reach Robert Mendez."

"This is Rob."

"Hey, Rob. It's Mike Cable. I'm returning your call about the job at Prospect High."

Well, what do you know?

It was a short but pleasant conversation. I decided to tell Coach Cable right up front about who I was and what made my application unique. Nowhere on my résumé or job application did it say anything about my physical condition, and I didn't want it to be a surprise down the road, in the event that I was fortunate enough to get an interview. What I'd forgotten is that I wasn't quite as anonymous as I'd once been. A year and a half had passed since the *Mercury News* had published its feature story, but apparently it had resonated with some people. Coach Cable was one of them.

"Yeah, Rob, I know who you are. I read the story, and I've seen you at clinics and tournaments. I know you can coach. Let's get together and talk about the job."

It took me a few seconds to formulate a response, but eventually I was able to spit out the words "Yes, sir" through a wide smile.

A few days later we met at Prospect, at the end of the day, when some of the players were finishing an off-season weight-training session. I was driven to the school by my caregiver at the time, a good friend named Mike, who'd started out as my landlord and then assumed the role of caregiver.

I'd applied for dozens of jobs over the years, but I felt more anxious than usual as I rolled up to the front door of Prospect High School.

I wanted this one. Bad.

The question was, did Prospect want me?

"To be brutally honest, when I first saw that—when Rob first rolled out—I said, 'How can this guy coach?'" Mike later admitted, when he was interviewed by ESPN. "We had a lot of applicants for the position, but as I got to know him a little bit, I just knew he would be a great fit for these young athletes."

I've never wanted anyone to give me a job out of sympathy. All I've ever asked for is a chance to show what I can do. Coach Cable gave me that opportunity, and I think his reservations melted away when he watched me coach. That's the way it usually works. After a little while, people forget that I'm in a wheelchair. I can communicate. I know the game of football. The other stuff kind of goes out the window because they realize I'm here to coach football. I'm not here to motivate or inspire—well, no more so than any other coach or teacher. If that happens, great! It's a by-product of doing the job right, of caring. But once we step between the lines, I'm here to coach football. It doesn't matter that I have no arms or legs. It doesn't matter that I've never played the game. The kids can feel my energy, my passion.

"I love this game of football!" I tell them. "And I love every one of you. We are a family."

I had made that introductory speech countless times, and the more I talked to Coach Cable, the more I hoped I would get the opportunity to deliver it to the kids at Prospect.

It was less an interview than it was a conversation, which I appreciated. Coach Cable seemed like a genuinely thoughtful and decent man, someone I'd want to hang out with off the field as well as on the field. He'd done his homework too.

"I know you're dialed in as far as the Xs and Os," he said. "You know the game. You know the playbook. You want to win. But I want to get to know you as a person. What do you want out of this job? What's important to you—beyond winning or losing?"

Man, I liked this guy. We were speaking the same language.

"My number one goal is getting the kids to work together as a team, to encourage each other, respect each other, and to care about each other. It's all about love."

Coach Cable said nothing, just kind of sat there for a moment, expressionless. Then, slowly, he began to smile.

"Yeah," he said. "Exactly."

The meeting wasn't enshrouded in incense and mist. We did get around to talking the nuts and bolts of football (because that's what football coaches do) and our respective expectations for the upcoming season. I talked about the spread offense, putting points on the board, getting kids to commit to a rigorous off-season training regimen. (That's a challenge for any program, and I was encouraged that at least today's weight-lifting session had been reasonably well attended.) And, since it's always a good idea for the applicant to be inquisitive, I asked Coach Cable what his top priority was.

"First of all, we have to make sure the kids take their studies seriously and stay academically eligible," he said. "That's a challenge."

Again, we were on the same wavelength. I had prepared a portfolio for the interview, and one of the things I had included was a suggestion that we hold the players accountable for academic success beyond what was even required by the school. So, if the school mandated a 2.0 grade point average as the eligibility standard, we'd set the bar higher.

"A 2.0 lets you be part of the team," I suggested, "but you're going to need a 2.5 if you want to start on game days. That way, the boys will know we're serious."

The meeting lasted about forty-five minutes, and it felt like we could have talked for another hour. Finally, Coach Cable said, "I think you're a good match for the JV team, and I'd like you to be the head coach."

WHO SAYS I CAN'T?

I was almost speechless, which doesn't often happen to me.

"Wow," I said, almost in a whisper. "Thank you."

"Well, it's not official," Coach said. "But I want to hire you. So just be patient. It might take a couple of weeks."

After the meeting, I rolled out of the school and across the street to a McDonald's to wait for my ride home. While there, I called my parents to share the good news. They put me on speaker, and I told them all about Coach Cable and Prospect High School, and how I was finally going to be a head coach. My dad was thrilled and proud. My mom had one question.

"Is the school in a nice area?" she asked. "Because we want you to be safe."

"Yes, mom. Very nice."

"That's good."

I laughed. "Love you guys."

CHAPTER NINE

few weeks passed as my application churned its way through the HR system. There was a formal interview with the Prospect High School athletic director, a background check, a review of references—all the usual due diligence. The actual hiring was almost anticlimactic. By that point I was already in head coach mode, planning strategy, an offensive playbook, off-season workouts. I couldn't wait to get started!

I owed someone a phone call first. I had promised Kristen Lappas that if I ever landed a head coaching job, I would let her know right away. It had been a long time since we'd talked, and I had no idea whether she was still interested in the story. To be honest, I didn't really care and felt somewhat apprehensive about calling; there was a self-promotional element to it that made me uncomfortable. Anyway, I was completely focused on coaching, and I worried that a documentary film crew might be intrusive. But a promise is a promise.

Kristen assured me that (1) ESPN was still interested in the project and (2) I would barely even notice their presence.

"You will get used to us," she insisted with a reassuring laugh. "And then it's like we're not even there."

At the time, that seemed hard to believe, but it turned out to be 100 percent true. Still, it wasn't just my feelings that merited concern. This was a feature story not just about a coach but a junior varsity football team, which meant ESPN was required to secure legal permission from the boys on the team, as well as their parents and the school administration. There was a lot of logistical legwork that isn't ordinarily part of the process when you're working exclusively with adults.

Although a year and a half had passed since Kristen and I first talked, the plan hadn't changed. She wanted to produce a short feature that would air on ESPN's *SportsCenter*. She warned me that even this short airtime would require a significant investment on the part of her and her crew. Producing a documentary is a bit like making maple syrup, with hundreds of hours of footage being boiled down to a few minutes of final product.

A few weeks before preseason practice started, I met some of the kids informally, at a weight-training session. It wasn't the most encouraging introduction, given that turnout wasn't as high as it should have been so close to the start of the season, and quite a few of the boys weren't taking it seriously. But I'd been coaching long enough to know this wasn't unusual at the JV level. Fifteen-year-old boys can be hard to corral; moreover, winning is a by-product of preparation and hard work, but until the winning begins, it's hard for kids to see the benefit. It's a difficult cycle to break. I didn't say much that day. I just kept working and planning, getting ready for the first day of practice.

In recent years, the JV team at Prospect had lost a lot more games than it had won, but I was confident I could help turn things around. I was excited about getting a chance to be a head coach and to use all the knowledge and experience I'd accumulated in the previous dozen years. I'm sure if you ask some of the kids on that team, they'll admit that when Coach Cable introduced me, they weren't sure what to think. Doubt and skepticism, and even discomfort, were understandable responses. Indeed, I later heard that a few kids decided not to stay with the program because they didn't want to play for a coach in a wheelchair. This may have been true, or it may simply have been that my presence gave them an excuse to quit. Football is hard. It's not for everyone. Regardless, I had endured the awkwardness of initiation many times before, and if I did my job, those feelings would dissipate.

So, when I looked out at a sea of blank pubescent faces on the first day of practice, I wasn't the slightest bit dismayed.

"I'm excited to work with you, gentlemen. Let's get started!"

Kristen and her crew traveled to the Bay Area a few times before we even played a single game, for about fourteen days total. Although it was true that their presence soon became like white noise, I was deeply impressed by the amount of research and reporting they were putting into what I assumed would be a short and quickly forgotten feature.

On the first trip, in late June, Kristen spent most of her time interviewing and filming members of my family, as well as some friends and an assortment of coaches with whom I'd worked over the years. She was extremely thorough. By the second trip, in late July, we'd begun preseason practices, and the atmosphere around the program had become progressively more serious. I love kids, and I can and do appreciate their quirks and often unfocused, hyperemotional demeanor. (I used to be one of those kids!) I want them to know I care, but I also know that it's not my job to be their friend. They have enough friends. From a coach, they want and need direction, discipline, re-spect, and mentorship.

You can care deeply about a young person without being a buddy. The friendship, with its implication of equal footing, comes later. I know this to be true, as I have friends who were once my teachers and coaches; I have friends whom I once coached. If I do my job, the relationship evolves and deepens. And my job is to be the adult in the room.

But I'm a work in progress, too, and I admit it can be difficult to strike precisely the right tone, to find the ideal balance between taskmaster and teacher. In the summer of 2018, I might have leaned too heavily on the former. I was a new head coach, determined to demonstrate I was up to the demands of the job. Some of the least effective coaches and teachers I've known have also been the seemingly nicest. They set minimal expectations and let the kids get away with minimal effort. They pat everyone on the back, clown around with their players or students, and end up accomplishing little. It's unfair to the young men and women and, ultimately, reflects badly on everyone involved.

There was another reason, as well, and that was my ego. I'm a highly competitive individual. I wanted to win games and prove I could coach as well as anyone, and that I wasn't a charity case. The team's performance—its attitude—would be a reflection of the head coach, and that was a very personal matter. But this is murky territory, for a coach should remember at all times that it's really not about him or her. It's about the players. It's about the kids. I wouldn't say I ever lost sight of that fact, but a few times during the preseason, my intensity probably seemed excessive to some players.

One hot July day, the boys were dragging, not paying attention and kind of going through the motions. This went on for about half an hour before I finally blew the whistle and stopped practice.

"Everyone in!" I shouted.

The kids straggled to the center of the field and formed a loose, sweaty circle.

"This is not a joke," I began. And then my voice began to rise. "If you don't want to be here, you can go home right now. I expect you to work your hardest! I expect you to care about each other!"

I yelled for several minutes, until my throat was raw and my voice was fading. I don't know if the boys were impressed or thought their new coach was out of his mind. But practice improved, and it continued to improve over the ensuing days and weeks. Mindful of something I had once heard about Bill Walsh, I was careful to keep my temper in check and not become an inveterate screamer. Walsh, the legendary coach of the San Francisco 49ers, had reportedly said that a coach had to be selective in unleashing outbursts. If you spend all day, every day screaming and yelling, turning red faced and howling at your players, they quickly tune you out.

Ah, that's just Coach, going on another rant.

But if you're generally calm but serious, and clearly in control, a well-timed outburst can have a profound impact.

Whoa, what's up with Coach? He's never like this. I'd better get it together.

So, as much as I was driven to win, as much as I wanted to prove what I could do, as much as I wanted my players to get the most out of this experience, I learned to bite my tongue. Which isn't to say that I tolerated a lack of effort or poor attitudes. I dismissed three players from the team during preseason workouts. They weren't bad kids, but they were, at that time, bad teammates. They clowned around, jogged through sprints, and for the most part acted as if they didn't want to be there.

Selfishness, apathy, laziness—these things can spread through a team (or any organization) like a virus. With no other option, I kicked all three players off the team. Expecting blowback, I wrote an explanatory note to the athletic director.

"This is not personal," I said. "But it's necessary at this time."

Additionally, I said the dismissal wasn't permanent. If the boys showed legitimate remorse and a sincere desire to return to the team—and this would be demonstrated in part by apologizing to their teammates—then they'd be welcomed back. A punishment of this type shouldn't be undertaken lightly by a new coach, as it can provoke serious consequences. Parents don't like it when their children are disciplined and commonly respond by marching into the school to demand a recount. But I heard nothing from the parents, which was encouraging, and by the time summer ended, all three boys had asked for a second chance.

"If you're ready to make it about the team, and not just about you, then we can move forward," I said. All three nodded. "Okay then."

None of the boys became a standout player or a model teammate. We had a few minor episodes related to effort and attitude as the season continued, but each was tamped down quickly and easily. There was improvement, both on the field and in the locker room. Kids aren't perfect, as none of us are. It's often two steps forward, one step back. The point is to keep making healthy progress toward the finish line, and to recognize and encourage that progress along the way.

By no means was I responsible for transforming the culture of a program. Prospect High School had a lot of terrific kids from solid families. There was a tradition of success in some parts of the athletic program, most notably baseball and soccer. Every school has sports that thrive and others that struggle. When I arrived, football was in transition. Coach Cable was a first-year head coach with a ton of energy and progressive plans. That he took a chance on me when he was the new guy himself says a lot about the kind of man he is. We shared a love for football and a firm belief that you put the well-being of the players ahead of everything.

The coaches I've admired have a vision for their programs, but they don't necessarily come in and rip everything apart and strike fear in the hearts of their players and staff. These coaches motivate by example. They take time to get to know their players—not just as athletes, but as students, and especially as young men. As I said, sometimes in the early days, I pushed the needle of intensity into the red zone, but I learned to back off and pick those moments carefully. Similarly, I tried to assess the team's strengths and weaknesses, and I relied on the players who brought not just skill to the roster but character as well. This isn't reinventing the wheel. Any new coach worth his whistle knows the importance of building camaraderie, and one of the best ways to do that is to find the natural leaders on your roster and get them to buy in to your philosophy.

I was lucky to have a few kids like that, including a tenth grader named Toa Tautolo. One of four siblings, and the youngest of three boys, Toa was a coach's dream: athletically gifted, mature, confident, smart. And humble. His father was a former US Marine. Every time I asked Toa a question, he'd respond, "Yes, sir."

"Toa, it's perfectly fine to address me as 'Coach,'" I assured him. "In fact, I kind of prefer it."

He nodded. "Yes, sir."

I sometimes worried that Toa was under a lot of pressure. When you're the youngest boy in a successful family, people have expectations you may be neither interested in nor capable of meeting. He was one of the school's best athletes; he also was a choir member and a strong student. I didn't push Toa hard because he always pushed himself.

"You're going to love this kid," one of the returning coaches, who was also a teacher, had said to me before the season, when we were analyzing the potential roster. "He will do anything and everything. He will run through a wall for you. He's all about team first, respecting his elders, and respecting his coaches."

Toa was a bit tall and lanky for the positions he played (fullback and middle linebacker), but he had toughness and a desire for contact. You could tell he would likely grow into his body, but for now he more than compensated through a combination of skill, hard work, and mental strength. Toa was one of our captains (of course), although I'm not sure the title was even necessary. He was the type of kid who naturally wanted to lead, and others naturally followed.

Like me, Toa could sometimes be so intense that it intimidated his teammates, and I had to pull him back. But I knew from the very first practice that we were lucky to have him on the team.

*   *   *

In August, following her second trip to the Bay Area, Kristen called to let me know that ESPN had changed its plans. The network no longer wanted to produce a short feature for *SportsCenter*. Instead, Kristen had convinced her bosses that the story merited more time and effort, perhaps a documentary of fifteen to thirty minutes.

"But we're going to need a lot more footage," she said. "If that's okay."

"Sure, I guess so," I said. "But why? I mean, what happened?"

Kristen explained that her initial attraction to the project stemmed primarily from my being a coach who overcame a great physical disability to pursue his dream. That alone was sufficient cause to pursue the story. But something happened during her second preseason visit. She said that the practices were much more intense and serious. She was struck by the sense that the players looked at me differently.

"They no longer saw you as a coach in a wheelchair. They just saw you as a coach. A coach who really cares.

And you obviously think of yourself that way too. That's the story I want to tell."

To tell the story properly, Kristen said she and her crew wanted to spend approximately a week per month during the season with our team. This had the potential to be a major imposition, so I ran it by Coach Cable first. As he had been when I'd first mentioned the project, he was supportive and open minded. He saw this as an opportunity to shine a positive light on Prospect High School and the football program. And I believe he trusted me to not mess it up, which I appreciated immensely. I also bluntly reminded the team of their responsibilities.

"Here's the deal," I began. "The ESPN crew is going to be here a lot. If you decide you want to be a showboat and act up for the cameras, you'll be gone so fast your head will spin. We are not here for the damn cameras. We're here for each other. I'll hold myself accountable, and I expect you to do the same. If you see a teammate doing something for the cameras, call them out. And if you want to call me out, well, that's okay too. Gentlemen, if this is going to hurt our season, we will shut it down."

It's interesting the way things worked out. I almost think that if the ESPN crew had come to only a few practices or games, it would have been more of a distraction. But they were around so often they became part of the scenery. After a while, we just stopped noticing. Also, thanks to social media, kids today are accustomed to being the stars of their own lives. For better or worse, they have grown up under a self-imposed microscope. You can bemoan the loss of innocence and debate how unhealthy it is to chronicle your life on Snapchat or Instagram, but it is what it is. A camera in the corner of a football field seems almost quaint by comparison.

Also, I trusted Kristen to do the job thoughtfully and professionally, to present a story that might help others who are facing challenges. It would be months before I knew whether that trust was warranted. In the meantime, we had a football season to play.

I was eager and confident, and the thirty young men on our team (the biggest JV roster Prospect had fielded in years) were improving every day. We didn't have a lot of size, so the spread offense worked to our advantage, and the kids enjoyed the freedom and explosiveness it offered. As August was about to give way to September, and the dawn of a new season, everything seemed to be going great.

And then, on August 26, 2018, I fell out of my chair.

• • •

That day at the hospital, all I could think about was how I'd let everyone down. Coach Cable had taken a chance on me. He had looked past my physical differences and straight into my heart and head. He hired me because of my résumé and references, not because he felt sorry for me. I'd convinced him I was every bit as reliable as any able-bodied coach. And I knew the game better than most of them.

Now, here I was, throwing up in the ER, stiches in my head, blood caked to my face, suffering from a concussion that threatened to sideline me for at least the first two weeks of the season, maybe much longer. All because I had fallen out of my chair.

I felt stupid.

I felt angry.

And by the time I got home Monday morning, I felt determined to prove the doctors wrong.

"Take as much time as you need," Coach Cable told me. "Don't worry."

I did worry, and not just for the generic reasons that any coach would fret about missing a practice or two weeks of practices. The reality of my physical situation factored into the equation and served as motivation. For one thing, I tried to picture Coach Cable or one of the assistants explaining to the team what had happened.

"Coach Mendez fell out of his wheelchair."

It sounded sad and pathetic. Worst of all, it sounded . . . *inevitable.* As if everyone should have realized that at some point, the coach with no limbs would have a terrible accident and be unable to fulfill the minimum requirements of his job. This was precisely the type of notion I'd been trying to dispel for most of my life. It was a freak accident, and it wasn't anyone's fault. Nevertheless, I felt as though I was at risk of proving the naysayers right, of setting back not just my own career but opportunities for others who face prejudice and doubt based merely on their appearance.

On a more basic but no less important level, I felt awful for our players. It wasn't their fault they had a coach in a wheelchair. I couldn't let them down. I also thought it might be a teachable moment. Football is a fun and beautiful game, but it is also undeniably *hard*. If I'm going to preach to kids about being strong, and working through pain and adversity, then I have to walk the walk (so to speak). I am compelled to demonstrate that I can handle adversity as well. I don't mean for that to sound nonsensical. Yes, most people would consider a normal day for me to be one that is endlessly challenging. But that's my normal, and I don't give it a lot of thought. What happened that evening in my parents' garage was way out of the ordinary. The resulting damage presented an opportunity for me to show my players not only that I cared about them but that I wouldn't hold them to a higher standard than I held myself.

So I took exactly as much time as I needed: one day. By Tuesday, I had returned to practice. I had a nasty headache, a black eye, and a badly swollen cheek. But in some ways, I'd never felt better.

"You think I look bad?" I said to the team that day. "You should see the garage floor."

They all laughed. Humor can diffuse almost any situation. That's something else I've learned.

Another thing I've learned—and maybe this is ridiculously obvious—is not to judge a book by its cover. Football is traditionally a game of size and strength. Big guys dominate, especially at the high school level. The Prospect JV team was undersized and overmatched, yet once I spent some time with our kids and got to know them, I knew we'd be all right. For one thing, they were tough as hell. For another, they were fast. It was impossible to know how things would play out, but I could tell this team had potential.

* * *

Two weeks later, we opened the regular season, against Santa Clara High School. This wasn't a game we were expected to win. We were both members of the West Valley League, but the league was divided into three divisions: A, B, and C. Santa Clara was the defending champion of the A division. We were in C, as usual, and coming off another losing season. Santa Clara had fifty-four boys on its JV roster. Although we'd begun preseason practice with thirty players, injuries and defections left us with an active roster of twenty-four on opening night. On paper, this was a complete mismatch between two teams at opposite ends of the West Valley League spectrum. A repeat of the previous year's game, won by Santa Clara by a score of 43–7, didn't seem out of the question.

Being a substantial underdog can work to your advantage, as long as your team isn't scared out of its mind at the prospect not just of losing but of being physically punished. Our kids weren't scared. It helped, too, that this was technically a nonleague game. Only games against opponents in the C division would count toward our division record and a potential C division title.

Yes, it was crazy to think of such things, given the program's history, but that's what opening night is all about: hope.

"The one thing I want to stress to you guys is honesty," I said before the game. "I want you to be able to look at yourselves in the mirror after this one is over and say, 'I went hard on every play.' If you can do that, then I don't care about the final score. Tonight is about effort—doing your best on every play."

A few of the boys nodded. Most sat stoically.

"And try to have fun," I added. "I don't mean laughing or clowning around. I mean try to enjoy yourself. You're playing football with your teammates, in front of your friends and family. Appreciate that. Have fun. Win or lose, we do it as a team."

More nods. A few guys smiled, patted each other on the back, exchanged fist bumps.

"All right, gentlemen. Let's go play some football."

Two hours later, we returned to the locker room on the losing end of an 18–13 decision that felt better than most victories I'd experienced. It was the most impressive loss I'd ever been around. Santa Clara was a football power; we were not. Though we didn't exactly celebrate in the locker room, a palpable buzz filled the air.

Hey, maybe we're not bad.

We were more than not bad. Over the next two months, the Prospect JV team won seven consecutive games, outscoring its opponents by a combined score of 151–32. Almost every week, our guys were smaller than their opponents. We had fewer players on the roster. We looked inferior. But like I said, appearances can be deceptive. We had a 110-pound quarterback who ran our offense beautifully, throwing on a dead sprint or off balance, and fearlessly taking hits from guys who outweighed him by a hundred pounds. We had an entire team of kids who were quick and tough and courageous, and who believed in and cared about one another.

Put all those things together, and you have a team that ends up playing for the JV championship of the

West Valley League, on October 27, 2018. Two of our best players so impressed Coach Cable that they were invited to move up to varsity. They chose to stay on the JV team, to play with their friends and teammates, and to finish what they'd started.

In the championship game we faced Sobrato, the same school where I'd coached briefly a few years earlier and where my tenure had ended badly. It's fair to say I felt like I had something to prove in that game. But ultimately, it wasn't about me. If you're a good coach, you know that. It's always about the kids. We lost the championship game, 3–0, the only points coming on a Sobrato field goal with 4:37 left in the game. I have to give that kicker credit. Field goals aren't common at the JV level, and in the closing minutes of a championship game, they're almost impossible. We had a chance to tie on our final possession, but a fourth-down pass was broken up, allowing Sobrato to run out the clock.

Our kids played their hearts out that day, and afterward, most of them cried. I did too.

"It's going to hurt today," I told them. "And that's okay if it hurts, because we cared a lot. We love this game of football. And we did this as a family."

The season was its own reward. Not just the victories, but the relationships—the communal struggle and the striving to be better, both as athletes and as people. Openly and generously caring for one another. Every day. I don't know any successful coach who isn't hypercompetitive, and I fall into that category, but the true rewards of coaching, particularly when working with adolescents, are those that can't be found on the scoreboard.

All I'd ever wanted was to be a head football coach, and I felt like my dream had come true.

CHAPTER TEN

hen the stillness of the predawn hours was broken by an alarm chirping, my first instinct was to silence the noise. Morning is a challenging time for me, and I tend to ease into it slowly and methodically, stretching my spine into shape, clearing the cobwebs through meditation, and preparing for the physical and mental rigors of another day.

It's a process, one that typically begins with the sunlight breaking through the curtains. But as I looked around the room, I saw only blackness. A glance at my smartphone revealed the time: 3:15 a.m.

What the . . . ?

And then I remembered: I'd sct my alarm so I could wake in the middle of the night to watch the world premiere of *Who Says I Can't?* At that point, I hadn't seen even one minute of footage. Although I continued to have tremendous faith in Kristen and her team, I'd be lying if I said I wasn't nervous about viewing the finished product.

My hope was that the story would ring true, that it would depict the hardship of my life without making me look pitiful or sad. I hoped I'd look like a football coach who happens to be in a wheelchair, not a guy in a wheelchair who happens to be a coach. I hoped my friends and family would approve of how they were portrayed. Most of all, I hoped the documentary would reflect the strength and love of the kids on our team, and that they would approve.

I understood the need to maintain editorial and artistic integrity, both of which might have been compromised had I been involved in the process. At the very least, Kristen explained, showing me a rough cut would only have served to heighten anxiety and fuel a desire to offer advice. I was the subject of the documentary, but it wasn't my project. It was ESPN's project, and I'd accepted that from the beginning. Once you agree to allow a documentary film crew to chronicle your life and work, you have zero control over the process. You simply hope that it turns out well.

And at 3:15 in the morning, before the birds have started singing and before the California sun has risen cheerily above the mountains—when darkness fills your bedroom and your back is aching—it's easy to feel pessimistic.

Although I'd not seen a single frame of the documentary, Kristen had kept me apprised of its progress. Two months had passed since the end of the season. After a period of rest and recuperation, I had begun to think about the following year, and how we might improve enough to win the JV championship. If you love the game, off-season can be tortuously long. You finish the last game exhausted from the intensity of the season and eager to catch up on sleep, watch a few movies, read a book or two . . . and inevitably, your mind begins to drift. You find yourself playing *Madden* with friends online or watching ten hours of NFL on Sunday. You find yourself randomly diagramming plays on your smartphone in the middle of the day or thinking about which of the two kids fighting for the starting quarterback job next summer is hitting the weight room right now.

You wake up one day and discover you're ready for the season to start.

And it's only December.

That's pretty much where I was when my alarm went off in the middle of the night.

You might reasonably wonder why the film premiered at such a ghostly hour, as if ESPN were trying to hide it. Which was exactly the case. Kristen and her team had been completely transparent with me about all of this. They wanted to wait until May, to unveil the documentary at the Tribeca Film Festival, but to be eligible for awards season, including the Emmys, it had to air before the end of the calendar year.

So it aired exactly once, in late December, in the middle of the night. And not on the flagship ESPN or even ESPN2, but on ESPNews, available only through an app downloaded either to your phone, laptop, tablet, smart TV or, in my case, PlayStation 4. It was the opposite of prime time.

The version of *Who Says I Can't?* that aired that night was thirty minutes long. The same version premiered at the Tribeca Film Festival in May the next year. A shorter, fifteen-minute version had premiered on ESPN in February and is now the only version available to the public. As I sat in bed that night, I didn't know the documentary remained a work in progress. It was the strangest feeling, to see myself on screen like that, and to see my family and friends and coaches speaking so earnestly. My biggest concern was that the film would be . . . what's the right word? *Cheesy.* I'd seen or read more than my share of "inspirational" stories that turned out to be almost embarrassingly clichéd or cloying.

"Please," I thought as the documentary began, "let it be good. Let it be . . . real."

It was certainly the latter of those two things, including the heartfelt interviews with my parents, who revealed personal feelings they'd never shared with me. It's quite a thing to watch your mom, who has always been such a ray of light, look out from a screen and admit through tears that she was so shocked by the sight of her newborn son that for the first two weeks, she barely saw him at all. Or to witness your father, who has always been so strong and supportive, admit that his first reaction had been to say to God, "What are we going to do with this boy?"

It struck me then that in the eyes of our parents, we never fully become adults. They never stop worrying, caring, loving. I was thirty-one years old, but to my mom and dad, the day I was born, a day of profound sadness and fear, still felt like yesterday.

So, yeah, it was real, all right. Scenes of my caretaker Mike picking me up like a baby and carrying me into the bathroom or helping me groom for the day, intercut with scenes of football games and practices and sideline chatter. And comments from our players that made me want to cry.

"Our opponents, they'd always doubt him," Toa Tautolo said. "Because they see a man in a wheelchair. To us, we see our coach, who's . . . perfect."

Man, I am pretty far from perfect. I'm just a guy trying to figure things out and do the best I can, but that any of the kids I coach would offer such an assessment—well, it was an overwhelming thing to see and hear.

Was the documentary good? To the extent that anyone who's the subject of a documentary can possibly offer an objective assessment, yeah, I thought it was good. It wasn't cheesy. But how would everyone else respond? By now, it was almost four o'clock in the morning. Had anyone seen it?

A few seconds after the closing credits rolled, my phone began to light up. There were calls from my mother and father, together on speaker. My dad choked up and my mom laughed nervously, which is what she does when she's so emotional that she can barely talk. There was a call from one of my uncles and texts from other relatives and friends, all of whom had either stayed up very late or risen very early. I told each of them, "Thank you for watching. I love you."

And I went back to bed.

Later that day, I reached out to Kristen to tell her what a great job she'd done and how much I appreciated it.

"It was so much better than I thought it would be," I said, realizing right away that what was intended as a compliment could have been construed as exactly the opposite. "I'm sorry," I quickly added, but Kristen just laughed.

I thought about how much work Kristen and her crew had put into the film—all the trips to the Bay

Area and the hundreds of hours of footage they'd accumulated. I tried to imagine how hard it must have been to pare it down to thirty minutes while maintaining a coherent and compelling narrative, one that told not just my life story but the story of the 2018 JV football team at Prospect High School. It had to have been like assembling the world's biggest jigsaw puzzle. But I recognize now that this is the task all documentary filmmakers face, and the good ones work incredibly hard and figure it out.

I was fortunate to have been in the hands of one of the good ones.

* * *

Not much happened for a while after that. ESPN's goal was to stealthily drop the documentary into awards contention and then quickly reel it back in. Mission accomplished. Aside from friends and family, and apparently a few people in Europe, who were revealed to me through social media, hardly anyone saw the premiere of *Who Says I Can't?* I went back to my quiet life, preparing for the upcoming football season and fielding the sporadic invitation to speak to church and youth groups.

It wasn't until mid-January, when trailers for the documentary began appearing on ESPN, that I got a sense of how my life might be affected. The trailer was interesting, if not downright oblique. It was intensely atmospheric, with a lot of shots of some crazy guy in a wheelchair yelling at kids playing football. I didn't know if it was a good commercial for the documentary or not. Would it frighten people away, or draw them in?

The latter, it seemed. Old friends and classmates began hitting me up on Facebook. Strangers reached out on Instagram.

"Dude, is this you?"

"Looks awesome!"

"Hey, Coach, when does this air?"

I wouldn't exactly call it *fame*, but it was definitely public exposure on a level beyond anything I'd known. The powers of ESPN and social media had combined to rock my quiet little existence, and it was only going to get louder.

In late January, I got an email from Kristen.

"We made a shorter version too."

Attached was a video file, a fifteen-minute version of *Who Says I Can't?* She explained that this version would be the version likely to air on ESPN in February, when it was finally, officially, unveiled to the public.

"Hope you like it."

I did like it. Very much. It was different, of course. Leaner and tighter. Arguably more exciting. The thirty-minute version had employed a neat narrative structure: five short "chapters," each narrated by a different person in my life. For the shorter version, that framing device had been jettisoned in favor of a more traditional approach, without a narrator. Honestly, I didn't care. I was just excited about seeing the documentary air on ESPN—on prime time. I wanted to see what my players and colleagues thought, since it belonged to them as much as it belonged to me.

•   •   •

By the time ESPN released *Who Says I Can't?* in February 2019, along with an accompanying feature story on ESPN's website and in the network's magazine (a shout-out here to Wayne Drehs, ESPN senior writer), I was deep into preparation for the next season. But the memories came rushing back, along with a tidal wave of publicity and media attention I hadn't anticipated, and for which I was completely unprepared. Every day seemed to bring another interview request. Friends I hadn't heard from in years reached out through social media, as did thousands of people I'd never met. I was approached by an agent who represented, among others, former NFL All-Pro wide receiver Donald Driver, himself a powerful motivational speaker and bestselling author.

"Your life is going to change," he told me. "I hope you're ready."

I was not ready.

I was just a football coach, and I was happy to remain "just a football coach." I had my dream job. I loved the kids at Prospect. What more could I ask for?

But some things are beyond our control. Sometimes life presents us with opportunities masquerading as obstacles. I'm an outgoing, friendly guy by nature, but suddenly it seemed that I couldn't leave the house without someone wanting to say hello and tell me how they were "inspired" by the ESPN film. At first it was flattering, and then it became almost overwhelming.

As I often do, I turned to the Bible for clarity and reassurance. Slowly, steadily, it began to dawn on me:

This is why I was born. This is why God put me here.

The acceptance of this role came gradually, but if I could point to a moment of clarity, it was the day I got a handwritten letter in the mail from a high school student with autism. By this time, I'd been getting a fair number of emails and messages through various social media platforms. But a handwritten letter is different. Not only is it a relic from another time, but it takes much more thought and effort than it does to bang on a few keys on your phone or laptop. Care goes into every word. Then you have to put the letter in an envelope, drive to the post office, buy a stamp, drop the letter in the mail. In comparison, it's easy to mindlessly scroll through emails and texts and DMs. But when a handwritten letter arrives, you pay attention.

As the months went on, lots of envelopes arrived, and I responded to as many as possible. But this letter stuck with me. Despite his autism and diminutive stature (he was only in ninth grade), this kid was a fitness freak who loved football and wanted to make the varsity team the next year. In a letter from his mother (included in the same envelope) was the startling revelation that the boy could bench press nearly two hundred pounds and that he'd been working harder than ever after seeing a story on ESPN about a man born with no arms or legs who had chased his dream of becoming a football coach.

"Your story has given him the courage to try out," she explained. "He wants to play linebacker."

I wrote back immediately.

"It doesn't matter what position you play," I said. "All that matters is that you're willing to work hard and try out."

Then there was the girl who wrote me a letter saying she'd been inspired by the accident in my parents' garage. I'd been mostly embarrassed about that episode, but her letter helped me see it in a different light.

"You fell out of your wheelchair, and two days later you were back on the field coaching football," she wrote. "That showed me that even after I broke my arm, I can go back to gymnastics."

Then, dramatically, she added, "Who says I can't? No one!"

More than anything else, these types of letters changed my whole attitude about fame and celebrity. At first it was kind of cool, then mostly intrusive. But now I see it as an opportunity, if not an obligation. If I can show by example that there's hope and possibility in this world, that's pretty great.

I never want to be defined by the things I don't have, and if my refusal to be limited by physical challenges serves as an inspiration to others, so be it. I'm okay with that. In fact, I embrace the role. What I don't want is for someone to look at me and feel pity or say, "Well, I guess I shouldn't complain. Look at that guy—his life really sucks!" My life doesn't suck. It's hard, but it's also beautiful. If I have a message, it's this: It's okay to feel bad. It's okay to feel pain and frustration.

The question is, what are you going to do about it?

The phrase *Who says I can't?* isn't intended as a denial of reality or a claim there's nothing we can't do if we put our minds to it. It's more about making the best of a situation and maintaining a positive outlook even in the face of difficult circumstances. For me, the most efficient and healthy way to go through my life—and to enjoy all that being alive entails—is to realize there will be things I can't do. But understanding that and accepting it isn't failure. I try to persevere through the things that aren't going to happen.

I am not going to walk. Ever. I am not going to do a lot of the regular stuff that everyone else can do.

There. I said it. It sucks sometimes, but it's the truth of my existence. Time to move on. Prioritize the things I *can* do rather than the things I *can't*. I'm not going to sit around at home, watching TV all day and collecting disability checks and feeling sorry for myself. That's not me; that's never who I've been. I need to be around people. I need to connect with them. Being active and social in the world taught me that while I couldn't *play* football, I could still be around the game and perhaps find a meaningful place in it. I could still be happy. I think that applies to a lot of different aspects of life. *Who says I can't?* is as much metaphor as an actual challenge.

Okay, maybe I can't do this particular thing, but not being able to do it will drive me even harder to do something else, to chase my own personal vision of happiness and success.

I guess you could say the phrase isn't like raising a giant middle finger to the world—it's more like opening your arms for a welcoming embrace.

CHAPTER ELEVEN

A s I looked out the window of the plane and saw the towering Manhattan skyline rising up to greet us, all I could do was smile and think, "In a year of 'firsts,' this is the biggest."

Here I was, traveling to New York City for the first time in my life, for the big-screen premiere of *Who Says I Can't?* at the Tribeca Film Festival. I was born and raised in Northern California; money and other logistical challenges have made traveling problematic for me, so I was thrilled to get a chance to visit New York. It was every bit as frenetic and exciting as I thought it would be. Not long after checking into our hotel on the Lower West Side, I made a point of steering my wheelchair down a busy Manhattan street, with traffic buzzing past in both directions, and screaming "Who says I can't?!" before a crowd of puzzled onlookers.

Now that was a popular Instagram post!

The best part about traveling to New York for the premiere was getting to share it with my family and friends. There were roughly a dozen us in the group: my parents and siblings; my caretaker, Mike; my manager, Memo; a couple of aunts; and my eighty-year-old grandmother, who turned out to be the life of the party, which was cool, if not entirely unexpected.

One of the things that struck me about Manhattan was how much it looked and felt and sounded exactly the way it did on TV or in the movies. The lights, the cars, the buildings, *the people*! I had lived in San Francisco's Chinatown for a while in my early twenties, so I wasn't entirely unfamiliar with urban density, but Manhattan is on a whole different level. It's big and loud and busy. People everywhere, elbow to elbow, heads down, rushing from one place to another with purposeful strides. I swear, if you slow down for even a second, you'll get swallowed by the humanity. The streets are like windswept canyons, walled off by buildings so tall you have to lean straight back to see the sky.

It was intimidating, exciting, beautiful.

By late afternoon on the day of the premiere, however, I'd begun to find the whole experience stressful. A combination of factors led to what I can only describe as a mild anxiety attack. For two days, I'd felt responsible for making sure everyone was having a good time and getting along. They did, with no more than the usual emotion or tension that runs through any large family gathering, especially one that culminates with everyone getting dressed up and attending a formal event. My mom kind of hovered over me, the way mothers do, while Kristen called and texted repeatedly to make sure everything was okay, and Memo kept reminding me of my various obligations throughout the night: red carpet, screening, question-and-answer session, after-party. All of this sounds awesome on paper (and it *was* awesome!), but as the day went on, I found it increasingly difficult to relax and enjoy the moment.

"I need to get out of here for a while," I told Memo.

He looked up from his phone. "What do you mean, 'get out of here'?"

"It's too crazy. I'm really stressed out, and I'm nervous about tonight."

"Tonight will be fine, Coach. You'll do great. Everyone is going to love the film."

"I just need some time to myself."

As long as I've known him—which has only been for a couple of years—Memo has been supportive in a hundred different ways. He eventually assumed caretaker duties from Mike, and he's been great at helping me build a marketing plan for the *Who Says I*

Can't? brand. But at that time, there was hardly a brand to speak of. I was still just a football coach trying to get used to the idea of being a semicelebrity, and some days it weighed on me. In those times, Memo provided a buffer, even if it meant keeping a secret from my family.

"Where are you going?" he asked.

"Not sure."

Memo tilted his head, smiled slightly. "Okay, well . . . you've got about an hour before the red carpet. Don't be late."

"I won't."

"Robert," he added, holding up his phone, "call me if anything happens."

I wound up at a dive bar on Second Avenue, ground level, right across the street from the Village East Cinema, which would be hosting the Documentary Sports Shorts program that night for the festival. I rolled through the open front door, wildly overdressed in a suit and tie, went straight to the bar, and ordered a beer. For a few minutes, I wanted to return to my old lifestyle, the one where no knew me, where I could go to a sports bar to wind down after practice and have some chicken wings and a beer and watch a baseball or football game on the big screen. Or I could go to a quiet little coffee shop and read, to clear my head for a while.

Before long I struck up a conversation with a guy on the stool next to me. He was probably in his mid-to.late thirties, with dreadlocks and a curious, affable nature. He had just gotten out of work. He seemed happy and content with the simplicity of his life, something I felt I might be losing. At one point, the bartender, a youngish woman with a chatty, New York sense of humor, asked me why I was all dressed up. I answered with a question.

"You know the Tribeca Film Festival?"

"Yeah, sure."

I hesitated, uncertain of how much to reveal.

"They're showing some sports documentaries this year, and I'm a big sports fan."

She nodded and walked away, which was a relief, because that was as deep into the conversation as I wanted to go.

"You like sports, huh?" the guy with the dreads asked. "What's your game?"

"Football, mainly."

He smiled. "Me too."

We talked about the NFL for a bit, and then he asked about the film festival. I sensed he knew something was up, that I wasn't being entirely forthcoming, or maybe he was just an inquisitive guy. Regardless, I've never been a good liar, so before long I told him the whole story, about how I was the subject of one of the films. He'd seen promos for the short version of

Who Says I Can't? that aired on ESPN, so I had looked vaguely familiar. He seemed happy for me, and his happiness, along with his entirely chill demeanor, helped put me at ease. The beer (just one, mind you) didn't hurt either.

After about forty-five minutes, I told him I had to get going. We exchanged phone numbers and social media information and promised to keep in touch (which we did).

"Good luck, Robert."

"Thanks." I leaned forward and stuck out my shoulder. "Give me a fist bump."

He reciprocated with a smile and a tap on the shoulder. "All right."

By the time I got out into the evening air, my phone was blowing up. Texts from my parents, from Memo, and multiple inquiries of escalating urgency from Kristen.

"Where are you?!"

I felt bad. This was a big night for Kristen—even bigger than it was for me. This was her project, the culmination of more than a year of intense work, and she had done an amazing job. I didn't mean to cause her any additional stress. I'd just needed a few minutes to breathe.

There was no point in responding to the texts, since I could see the theater from outside the bar, a crowd gathering on the red carpet. It was only about

a hundred yards away (the length of a football field!),
so I shifted into overdrive and rolled across the street.
When I pulled up, Kristen was taking pictures with
her family. Memo caught my eye first. He walked over,
smiled thinly, and leaned down.

"You're late, buddy."

"Yeah, I know. Sorry."

I was only about ten minutes behind schedule,
which was inconsiderate, but not fatal. And at least I
was in a much better mood, the anxiety replaced by
appreciation. Looking around the theater, at all these
people gathered to watch a series of short sports
documentaries, including one that was about my life,
I felt humbled. And grateful.

The screening ended with a crowd of a few hundred people standing and cheering. There was a
brief question-and-answer period with the audience,
enthusiastically moderated by Kristen, and then off
we went to an after-party (arranged by Kristen and
my agent, Brian Lammi) at a nearby nightclub, with
everyone dancing and laughing and eating and
drinking. I finally got to meet Kristen's family, which
was wonderful, especially since she'd already gotten
to know mine so well. I talked with various ESPN
editors and other people who'd worked so hard
behind the scenes. There was, for example, one au-
dio technician I'd spoken with on the phone a few
times a week for eight months. But until that night,

we'd never met in person. Throughout the filming, this guy was always asking me, "Coach, can you lower your voice a little? It's overpowering the microphone."

To which I'd reply: "You do work for ESPN, right?"

"Uh-huh."

"So . . . you know football coaches yell a lot?"

Then we'd both laugh. Like everyone else involved in the project, the guy had seemingly endless patience and immeasurable skill, a fact revealed once again as I watched the film on a big screen for the first time. I was awestruck by how much work went into this half-hour documentary and by the level of professionalism and commitment everyone brought to the project.

● ● ●

The next day, we all traveled from New York to Bristol, Connecticut, to visit ESPN's sprawling campus. Ostensibly, the trip up I-95 was an opportunity to glimpse behind the curtain. If you're a sports fan in America, like I am, then ESPN is much more than an acronym or a TV station (or collection of TV and radio stations and podcasts and streaming outlets and various other modes of content production and distribution). ESPN is, and has been for more than four decades, "the worldwide leader in sports." For me, and for anyone who lives and breathes sports, getting a chance to visit ESPN headquarters is like a kid getting the chance to go to Disney World.

There was, in fact, a specific reason for the invitation. ESPN had determined that I was under consideration to receive the Jimmy V Award for Perseverance at the annual ESPY Awards, which is sort of like the Oscars for sports. The Jimmy V Award is, in many people's eyes, the most prestigious of the ESPYs, although it's not something you achieve through normal athletic means, like winning a championship or performing at an extraordinarily high level. Instead, it's presented to "a deserving member of the sporting world who has overcome great obstacles through perseverance and determination." The award is named after the late, great North Carolina State basketball coach and popular broadcaster Jim Valvano, whose unforgettable acceptance speech upon receiving the Arthur Ashe Courage Award at the 1993 ESPY Awards brought a Madison Square Garden crowd to its feet and moved millions of viewers to tears. Suffering from terminal cancer, Jimmy V fought through the pain and delivered one of the most memorable speeches in sports history.

Hell, in all of history. Period.

I was too young to see the speech in real time, but I'd viewed it hundreds of times and always found it incredibly moving. I committed much of it to memory and even posted it on my website a few years ago. Here's the part that most resonates with me.

> When people say to me, How do you get through life or each day? it's the same thing. To me, there are three things we all should do every day. We should do this every day of our lives. Number one is laugh. You should laugh every day. Number two is think. You should spend some time in thought. Number three is you should have your emotions moved to tears, could be happiness or joy. But think about it. If you laugh, you think, and you cry, that's a full day. That's a heck of a day. You do that seven days a week, you're going to have something special.

That's it. Right there. That's the part I love and remember and repeat to myself when I'm feeling down. Not the part that most people recall—the part where Jimmy shouts, "Never give up!" That part is obvious. It's in my DNA, and in the DNA of any fighter. But this part here, the part about laughing, thinking and, especially, crying? Every day? It's brilliant. It's profound. And it's so true. I tell my players all the time that it's okay to cry. Crying means you care. You love.

Don't be ashamed of it. Rejoice in it.

You're human.

Coach Valvano's legacy lives on not just in the ESPY Awards or in a quarter-century-old video clip, but in the V Foundation for Cancer Research. The men and women who have received the award named in his honor all displayed courage and tenacity in the face of sometimes crushing adversity. Some, like Hall of Fame quarterback Jim Kelly and broadcasters Craig Sager and Stuart Scott, were famous. Others were less well-known. Many of the recipients had battled serious illness. Some are still battling. Some have lost. Some had been born with physical challenges and gone on to achieve greatness in the athletic arena. Others had once accomplished greatness, only to suffer devastating career-ending and life-threatening injuries.

I had a hard time figuring out where I might fit in with this group, but I tried not to think about it too much. The idea that others found inspiration in the very fact of my existence was still hard to comprehend. I got up in the morning and went to work. I coached my players to the best of my abilities. I did this from a wheelchair, and without arms or legs, which I guess some people find extraordinary. To me, it's just life. I do the best I can.

Maybe that's the definition of perseverance.

When I went to Bristol, I wasn't supposed to know I was on the short list of people under consideration to receive the Jimmy V Award, but Kristen had already let it slip during one of our conversations several weeks earlier. She was so excited for me and for the documentary. And I was happy for her. I wouldn't have been considered for the award if not for Kristen's incredible work on *Who Says I Can't?* So, in a very real sense, we'd be sharing in any honor that stemmed from its production.

"I think it's going to happen, Rob," she said. "But please keep it in-house for now. It's not official, and it's supposed to be a secret."

Still, when I visited the office of ESPN president Jimmy Pitaro—"You're going to Jimmy's office?" several ESPN staffers had exclaimed as I toured the campus. "Nobody gets to go up there."—and he officially broke the news, in front of my family, I was nearly overcome with emotion. We made small talk for a few minutes, and then, with an ESPN camera crew filming, Jimmy turned serious.

"Every year we have an event called the ESPYs," he began. "It's very important to us, to our company. As a part of that we celebrate the best in sports."

I knew where this was going, and suddenly I found it hard to breathe. I listened, nodded.

"The Jimmy V Award recognizes perseverance," he continued. "I just want to take a moment and congratulate you—you will indeed receive that award this summer."

As my sisters and parents gasped and began to cry, and as light applause filled the room, I let my head fall forward and closed my eyes, trying hard to maintain my composure. Knowing that it was possible, if not likely, that the visit would end with this exact revelation had done nothing to mitigate the emotion of the moment. But I had to speak—there were cameras, after all.

"Never give up is something I've always related to," I said, choking out the words. "It's just very humbling. Thank you so much, from the bottom of my heart. This is my Super Bowl, for sure."

"Thank you for letting us tell your story," Jimmy said.

There were lots of tears and hugs and fist bumps in the room. My father, who tries to hide emotion behind stoicism, leaned in and wrapped his arms around me and would not let go. I think it was the longest embrace of our lives, which is saying something.

By the time we left Jimmy's office, I'd begun to experience a powerful sense of the world having shifted. It was as if my life no longer belonged only to me; I was part of something bigger. I felt pride, but I also felt the weight of responsibility. I tried to imagine what it would be like to be at the ESPYs and receive the Jimmy V Award. I tried to picture myself going out on stage and speaking to millions of people.

Then I thought about what it would be like to mess up, and I started shaking. I pushed the image out of my brain and finished the rest of my tour in virtual silence, as I tried to process what had just transpired.

• • •

The next two months passed in a blur. The announcement of the Jimmy V Award brought more media attention and more viewers to the documentary. Suddenly, it was early July, and there I was, packing for a flight to Los Angeles, where the ESPY Awards would be held. I'd been assigned a writer who worked at ESPN to help me prepare a speech, a talented guy named Aaron, who had assisted the previous five winners of the Jimmy V Award. We'd talked several times, but I kept procrastinating, putting it off, avoiding the hard work of putting words on paper. Finally, the speech—part of it, anyway—came to me one day, and I called Aaron and began talking from the heart. It was like the words came straight from God. The message was so obvious.

"I want to urge people to focus on what they can do, not on what they can't do," I explained. "That's the story of my life."

"Sounds good," Aaron said. "Let's do it."

Approximately twenty of my friends and family members made the trip to Los Angeles to attend the ESPYs. I flew down a couple of days earlier with Mike and Memo. We stayed at the JW Marriott Los Angeles L.A. Live, a huge office and entertainment complex near the STAPLES Center. Within the complex is the seven-thousand-seat Microsoft Theater, where the ESPY Awards would be held.

The next day's rehearsal was almost more intimidating than the actual event. I don't know why—perhaps because I had a vague idea of what the ESPYs would be like, having watched the ceremony so many times on television. And I figured I could count on adrenaline to carry me through. But the rehearsal? That was a mystery. I decided to show up and do as I was told. My strategy was to try to blend into the background. The ESPY Awards attracts hundreds of famous athletes and celebrities from the entertainment world. Who would even notice me?

A lot of people, as it turned out, which, again, was more than a little disorienting. Before I'd even left the hotel, I ran into Adrian Peterson, the All-Pro running back for the then Washington Redskins.

"Hey, Coach!" he shouted. "Mind if I get a picture with you?"

"Uh . . . I think I'm the one who should be asking for a picture with you," I stammered. "But sure. Let's do it."

At rehearsal, I was approached by quarterback Russell Wilson, who's won about everything you can win in the NFL: Rookie of the Year, Super Bowl, six-time Pro Bowler. I had a long talk with defensive end Chris Long, who had recently retired after spending eight years in the NFL. I had admired Chris as a player but even more as a person. In 2015, he'd started a foundation to help bring clean water to communities in

East Africa. Two years later, he announced he would donate his entire 2017 season NFL salary to charity. Each week, his paycheck went to a different cause. This was an astonishing act of generosity, one that led to Chris's receiving the league's Walter Payton NFL Man of the Year Award in 2018. But what I realized, after talking with Chris and getting to know him a little, is that he doesn't do anything for publicity. He's a genuinely decent, philanthropic man who embraces life and wants to make the world a better place. And he doesn't mind rolling up his sleeves and working to get the job done.

To have a guy like that congratulate me and tell me I'm some sort of inspiration to him? That meant so much to me, but it was also a bit surreal.

I'd like to say I breezed through the ESPY Awards like a seasoned pro, but that wouldn't be true. I was a recipient of one of the featured awards, and because of the challenges involved in navigating from table to stage, my entire group was seated at the front of the theater, a few feet from the podium. As the parade of polished presenters and impeccably groomed recipients went by—Bill Russell, Patrick Mahomes, Giannis Antetokounmpo, the entire US National Women's National Soccer Team!—I could feel my heart pounding.

He looks great.

She sounds perfect.

I'm screwed!

Multiple times during the program, my father had to wipe the sweat from my face and forehead. It was pouring into my eyes. I worried that wet spots on my suit would be visible on TV.

About twenty minutes before the Jimmy V Award was to be presented, Memo and I were ushered backstage to a waiting area. It was a few feet from the stage, separated by a curtain, with a large-screen TV projecting the ceremony, so we could see and hear everything that was happening.

"Memo," I said. "I have to go to the bathroom."

Memo is cool, almost unflappable. He's a marketing and management genius who moved to the Bay Area from San Diego for the better part of a year to help me get a handle on the business opportunities that have come my way. But that request, at that moment, threw him.

"Now?" he said, his eyes flicking from the TV screen to the curtain, as a stopwatch ran in his head. "You have to go *now*?"

I nodded. "Yeah. I'm sorry."

A lifetime spent confined to a wheelchair has given me a degree of control over bodily functions that most people cannot imagine. I'm careful about what I eat and when I eat or drink. I try to make sure I use the bathroom before I leave the house, to avoid having to ask for help in a public situation. Most of the time, it's not an issue. I can hold it for a long, long time.

But right then, despite being dehydrated from sweating buckets all night, I had to use the bathroom. Urgently. It was part of the fight-or-flight response, I suppose—like a racehorse emptying his system in the starting gate before a race.

"Okay," Memo said. "Let's make it quick."

We did. A few minutes later I was back in the on-deck circle, hanging out with, among others, Dwyane Wade, Rob Gronkowski, and Lindsey Vonn, and continually thinking, "How did I get here?"

Then, it was just me and Memo. And finally, just me, as Memo stepped away to give me time to focus, to put my game face on. My name was announced, and off I went, from behind the curtain to out on the stage. There was a roar of applause and then . . .

A standing ovation?

For me?

I saw my parents and my sisters, smiling through their tears, and I felt a surge of strength. I wouldn't say the nervousness melted away, but it did subside somewhat. For the next four minutes, I spoke from the heart (with the help of a teleprompter, of course). I thanked my friends and family, my Lord and Savior, Jesus Christ. I thanked the players and coaches and administration at Prospect High School. And I thanked the game of football, which has given me so much over the course of my life:

If there's any message I want to give you guys tonight, it's to look at me, and see how much passion I've put into coaching and how far it's gotten me. When you dedicate yourself to something, and open your mind to different possibilities, and focus on what you can do, instead of what you can't do, you really can go places in this world. Realizing that I couldn't play football, but I could coach football, that was a way for me to never give up. From the words of Jimmy V—that was my way of focusing on what I can do. The best part of coaching, for me, is seeing someone's potential, and helping them realize what's possible. For anyone out there, not sure if they can do something—it can be in sports, it can be in your job, it can be in your life. Whatever it is, I'm here to tell you that you can do it. You've got to be passionate; you've got to work at it. But it can happen. And I'm not done yet. I've made it this far, and who says I can't go further. That's my message tonight.

I paused, not so much for dramatic effect, but to take a deep breath for the big finish.

And then I emptied my lungs. I yelled so loudly that they could hear me not just in the back row of the Microsoft Theater, but all the way up in Northern California, where we ended every practice the same way at Prospect High School.

"Who says I can't?! Nobody! Yeahhhhhhh!"

EPILOGUE

had no intention of hitting the pause button. It just sort of happened. I guess I should know better than most people that some things in life are beyond our control, but nevertheless I was caught off guard when much of the world shut down amid a global pandemic. Suddenly, after two years on a treadmill, there was time for reflection. Time for considering what is truly important in life.

A little background.

The ESPY Award led to more publicity: a mushrooming of followers on my social media accounts; congratulations from people I'd never imagined would know my name (Tom Brady? Really?); invitations to speak in front of corporate and educational audiences; appearances on national television and radio shows.

Like anyone else who has fame thrust upon him, I learned on the fly and did the best I could.

First and foremost, I was a football coach. A few weeks after the ESPYs, we began preseason practice at Prospect High School, where I returned as head coach of the junior varsity squad. We weren't quite as strong or talented as we'd been the previous year, but our numbers improved, and we had a great group of young men committed to the principles of sacrifice and teamwork and family, and who had totally bought into the program's offensive system. And in the end, our 2019 season was a virtual repeat of 2018. A narrow loss in the opener to powerhouse Santa Clara and an overall record of 8–2. A loss in week eight precluded playing for the league championship, but it was a successful and enjoyable season nonetheless, and I considered it a privilege to coach several of these players for a second consecutive season. I'm confident they'll do well on the varsity level, and in life.

I did, however, bite off a little more than I could chew over the course of that season, and by the end, I was completely exhausted. For one thing, I was no longer merely a football coach, or a coach who worked part-time at a call center. In addition to coaching, I had accepted a job as a teacher's aide.

Like most schools, Prospect preferred that its coaches were full-time employees of the school district. There are myriad reasons for this, most of them logical and understandable. The more time you spend around kids, the better you get to know them. It could be argued that a coach who interacts with students during the regular school day is more likely to have a fuller relationship with those students when they step on the practice field. The new principal encouraged me to seek this opportunity and fully supported the endeavor, despite the fact that some doubt and skepticism would be unavoidable, just as it had been when I was first named JV football coach.

In the same way I'd admired Mike Cable for having the courage to hire me when he was brand new at the job, I appreciated the new principal taking a chance. Both of these men displayed strength—not because I was likely to screw up, but because they were bound to face some questions and criticism stemming from others' preconceived notions. It's hard enough to be a new head coach, and harder still to be a new principal, without inviting controversy. But some people don't mind the heat; they're different—guided by a steadier moral compass. And thank God for that. It's one of the things that makes life so beautiful. If we were all the same, what a dull and sad world it would be.

There was just one problem with taking the job: it was a lot harder than I'd anticipated.

I was no stranger to working with kids, but working with kids for eight hours in a classroom, followed by two or three hours on the football field? Five days a week—plus a sixth day of practice, plus film review, coaching staff meetings? Here's what I think: teachers deserve to be paid better.

My job was to work primarily with ninth- and tenth-grade students, some of whom I also coached, helping them with their homework, making sure they were on task in the classroom, staying focused and attentive and respectful. The irony of this wasn't lost on me—a dozen or more years earlier, I'd been one of the kids who needed someone like me hovering over them, making sure they were getting their work done, rather than playing the class clown. I don't know—maybe that made me an ideal candidate for the job. I knew exactly how some of these kids felt.

It was enjoyable, rewarding, and important work, but after a couple of months, I was exhausted. For me, each day begins with a significant period of stretching and acclimation to ease the discomfort and tightness that comes with scoliosis. I have disc issues in both the cervical and lumbar regions of my spine, in addition to the scoliosis. I have nerve damage and muscle weakness. To some extent, much of my daily life revolves around pain management—how much can I tolerate without having to scale back activities? At what point is the risk of further damage greater than the benefit of constantly moving at warp speed and trying to fill every minute with pursuits that bring me joy, that allow me to be of service to others?

There is no easy answer, but I do know that without the morning preparation, I have a hard time getting through the day. It also takes me longer to get bathed and groomed and fed and dressed, and to commute to work. The school graciously offered me a start time one hour later than most employees, but with football practice after school, I still found that I was away from home for nearly twelve hours a day.

To my agent's chagrin, I had virtually no room in my schedule to accept public-speaking engagements or other business opportunities. I knew my body well enough to acknowledge I was already close to the breaking point and that, at minimum, I'd be short-changing my players by not being able to offer them 100 percent commitment and energy.

One exception I did make during the season was a trip to New York City, to appear on the *Rachael Ray Show*. That turned out to be a wonderful experience, not merely because of the exposure it afforded a budding public speaker, but because she generously arranged for the sporting goods manufacturing company Riddell, in partnership with USA Football, to donate $10,000 in equipment to the Prospect High School football program.

On a personal note, Rachael also arranged for a $10,000 grant, through the NFL Foundation, that I could apply to the cost of a new wheelchair, as well as a donation from Radisson Hotels, to defray the cost of lodging when I have to travel for corporate or speaking engagements.

When I was booked for the appearance, I didn't know any of this was coming. I had merely heard great things about Rachael and her show, and I was excited about getting another chance to briefly visit New York. By the time I left her studio, I was a speechless, teary-eyed mess.

With the end of football season came a transition into a more corporate world, and an ever-expanding series of opportunities that once would have seemed unimaginable. I was asked to speak to members of the Green Bay Packers and San Francisco 49ers. I was invited to the Super Bowl, where I got a chance to polish my interviewing skills and hang out with athletes and broadcasters I'd previously known only through their televised exploits. I spent a lot of time in planes and hotel rooms. There were more offers than I could accept.

And suddenly, everything came to a stop, and many of us became citizens of a strictly online world. Like it or not, there was time to think, to assess, to take stock.

I want to be clear on this: money isn't the most important thing in my life; never has been, never will be. I'm a firm believer in the old adage that if you choose a job you love, you'll never work a day in your life. Better still, if you're good at what you do, eventually you'll be rewarded. Coaching football is like that for me, and

I don't plan on ever giving it up. I'd love to be a head coach at the varsity level. I'd love to coach in college. Or even the NFL. Sound crazy? I don't think so.

Who says I can't?

But when you live your life in a wheelchair, practical considerations must be addressed. I've been fortunate to have opportunities to expand my role as a public speaker. With each appearance, I've gotten more comfortable on stage. Judging by audience responses, I guess I have a message that people want to hear. I'm honored and flattered to be of service, and I hope to turn what once was a modest side gig into something more substantial. Obviously, that's appealing in part because, well, let's be honest: my life is extraordinarily expensive. The medical costs, the adaptive equipment (motorized wheelchairs and vans, for starters), and the caregiving. Believe me, it adds up. The undeniable truth is that money buys freedom, security, and *independence*. That's the cold, unforgiving reality.

But it isn't all about money. Not by a long shot. My dream hasn't changed—it has broadened. When I say I want to be a successful motivational speaker, a bestselling author, and a great football coach, it's not because I'm driven by wealth or notoriety. I want to reach people. I want to inspire them to live their lives to the fullest, to never give up on their dreams and aspirations. And to love themselves for who they are.

Every so often, someone asks me if I've ever thought about getting prosthetic limbs. Of course I have. But it's not a simple thing. Typically, a prosthesis is attached to a portion of an arm or a leg, or at least a socket. It can be applied or removed in a matter of seconds, almost like putting on a shoe. But I have no limbs at all—not even a tiny nub. There is nothing to act as a conduit for the prosthesis. In my case, therefore, a prosthetic arm would have to be surgically attached, with the device electronically wired to the nerve endings in my shoulder.

For the longest time, this was the stuff of science fiction. When I was kid, for example, the technology wasn't sufficiently advanced to make it worth the risk. And the cost was prohibitive. I have greater resources now, and the technology has improved dramatically, but the basic formula still applies: deeply invasive surgery, followed by a long recovery and a steep learning curve. I'd have to learn many basic functions all over again. I mean, I can draw up a play on my smart phone using my teeth and a stylus faster than most coaches can draw one using a whiteboard and a marker. Surgically implanted prostheses would set me back about twenty years. And that's if they work at all—if my body doesn't reject them from the outset.

When I was in my early twenties and involved in a serious relationship, I thought about getting prosthetic limbs. The possibility of getting married and having children led me to strive for a more "normal" life. Not so much for myself but for those I loved. Interestingly, my girlfriend was opposed to the surgery, and not just because of the risks involved.

"I don't think you should do it," she said. "You wouldn't be you with arms and legs. It would change your whole persona."

She and I eventually went our separate ways, but her words have stayed with me. She was right. This is who I am.

Even on the hardest of days, I feel blessed. I'm here for a reason . . . and I'm not going anywhere.

ACKNOWLEDGMENTS

This book is based on my life and how it has evolved, from my upbringing to the present. I have many to thank for guiding and supporting me along the way. The support and love these people have given me is truly what keeps me going.

I'll begin by expressing my deepest gratitude for my Grandpa Danny and Grandma Mona, for the love they had for our family. To this day, they're both the most selfless people I know, and they'd do anything for us. They are the rock of our family, and I'll always have a soft spot for Salinas because of them.

My two sisters, Jackie and Maddy, thank you for your love and support. Jackie, as my older sister, was there for me a lot and was my best friend as a child. She always thought of how to include me in things, even though she knew I had limited capabilities compared to the average kid. We are all blessed by and grateful for her husband, Michael, who has been a great husband to Jackie, a great son-in-law, and beyond a great father. And to my beautiful nieces, Emma and Lily, thank you for bringing love and happiness everywhere you girls go. Thank you to my younger sister, Maddy, for inspiring me by being strong and independent.

I'm also blessed to have had my Tia Cindy and Tia Tota as part of my life when I was growing up. I am who I am today because of my family.

I'd like to acknowledge all of my friends from my hometown, Gilroy, and the whole Bay Area, whom I've shared many laughs with, as well as everyone else I've met along the way. Thank you to my close friends Alex, Abed, and Dominique, and my beautiful girlfriend, Janell, for always pushing me for the better and wanting the best for me.

I owe much gratitude to Kathi Visperes and Coach Pete Pedroza. Mrs. V was my one-on-one aide through elementary school to my junior year of high school. I appreciate her belief in me since day one. Coach Pete was my adaptive physical education coach. He worked with me from when I was a toddler until I was in high school and continues to encourage me. I'm very grateful for both of them.

I'm blessed to be able to coach and work with many great students, and I'd like to thank each and every one of them for their efforts and for allowing me to be a part of their lives for a short period of time. Thank you to my high school football coaches and later colleagues—Coach Bloom, Coach P, Coach Lemos, and Coach Yafai—for introducing me to the best job in the world: coaching American football.

Thank you to Coach Mike Cable for hiring me on to his staff and giving me my first head coaching job. I also want to thank everyone else from the Prospect community for allowing me to share my story with the world during my time at Prospect.

I would like to express my appreciation to my brother from another mother, Memo, for guiding and supporting me on this new journey, as well as my friend and marketing agent, Brian Lammi, for believing in me to do anything. Thank you to Carley Sanfilippo for helping me coordinate events and always reminding me how inspiring I can be. Donald Driver is also someone I'd like to acknowledge, as someone who has believed in me and guided me on this journey. And thank you to the rest of the Lammi family.

I also want to give a big thank you to Joe Layden, who helped me write this book. Joe invested a lot of time in helping me put my thoughts and feelings on paper, and he did an amazing job of helping me share my life story with all of you. I appreciate Frank Weimann for his efforts in finding the publishing company, HarperCollins, and connecting me with Joe.

I'd like to acknowledge and thank ESPN network for sharing my story through the documentary. And I would like to acknowledge Kristen Lappas for the hard work and dedication she put into making the documentary. I'm very grateful for her support, hard work, and friendship. I also want to thank Wayne Drehs for his great work in the making of the documentary.

I'm grateful for HarperCollins for publishing my first book. There's a lot of work and time that goes into writing a book, and I deeply appreciate everyone's help, dedication, and guidance throughout this whole project.

Lastly, I'd like to acknowledge and express how grateful I am for the love and strength the Lord gives me day in and day out. God bless you all.

ABOUT THE AUTHORS

oach **Rob Mendez** was born with an extraordinarily rare condition called tetra-amelia syndrome. He has no arms or legs and moves with the assistance of a custom-made, motorized wheelchair that he operates with his back and shoulders, and diagrams football plays on a smartphone, using a stylus that he maneuvers at lightning speed with his mouth.

Rob was a fixture on the Bay Area high school football coaching scene for more than a dozen years before moving to Southern California. He is currently the head junior varsity coach at a high school near San Diego.

A busy and accomplished motivational speaker, as well as a successful coach, Rob has been the subject of dozens of profiles in national media, as well as the ESPN documentary short feature *Who Says I Can't?* The film was nominated for a 2019 Emmy Award and was entered in the Tribeca Film Festival.

In the summer of 2019, Rob was named the winner of the Jimmy V Award for Perseverance at the ESPY Awards. After more than thirty years, he continues to beat the odds and serve as an inspiration for people worldwide who are facing adversity.

Joe Layden is an award-winning journalist and a multiple *New York Times* bestselling author. He lives in California.